TOPICS OF RESTORATION COMEDY

TOPICS OF RESTORATION COMEDY

by

DONALD BRUCE

LONDON
VICTOR GOLLANCZ LTD
1974

© Donald Bruce 1974

ISBN 0 575 01804 6

Printed in Great Britain by
The Camelot Press Ltd, Southampton

To Anselma Bruce

CONTENTS

PREFACE

I HOPE THAT this book will contribute something towards the respect for Restoration Comedy—which is, of course, not an organic whole, but an aggregate of individual and often differing writers—recently renewed by such patient and sensitive scholarship as that devoted to Congreve by Hodges, to Aphra Behn by Cameron, and to Shadwell by Sutherland. My special interest has been to present Restoration Comedy as a debating comedy, and as morally purposeful within its debates. Except in the historical and biographical introductions, I have disregarded critical writings. Already too many studies of Restoration Comedy have been about its critical reputation.

I would like to thank Professor James Sutherland, Professor W. A. Armstrong and Professor Beatrice White for giving me the opportunity to make the researches upon which this book is founded; Professor James Kinsley for kind advice about the text of John Dryden, and Professor Harold Brooks for the many things I have learned from him on other textual matters and questions of attribution; the undergraduates in my classes at Westfield College—particularly the bright progeny which graduated in 1972—for their stimulating discussion and appraisal of some of the views that follow; and Miss Sheila McIlwraith for her care in preparing the book for the press. My chief helper (here in writing this book, as everywhere) has been my wife, to whom the book is gratefully dedicated.

WESTFIELD COLLEGE, HAMPSTEAD   D. B.
OCTOBER, 1973

CHAPTER ONE

Cupid's Fav'rite Nation:
The Restoration and the Comedy

ON 25 MAY, 1660, the *Royal Charles*, once called the *Naseby*, arrived in sight of Dover. The royal Charles himself was on board, returning from exile, his face gaunt from his years of ineffectuality and sotting: a long-shanked royalty, spinning to all sides in a coil of blackamoor ringlets—mobile in his excitement. What plunder rose to his hands, what linked spoil of coy gold and enamelled nubilities! And Dryden gives us his word for it that the cliffs of Dover, white with sorrow and penitence, stepped forth to meet the ship.[1] The event is pictured at Hampton Court, in a portrait of the nautical and patient king, awash in a spume of importunate sea-nymphs. Samuel Pepys was on the spot, as often happened, being one of the king's escorts from Holland. So restless was the king, Pepys notes, that he ate for breakfast "nothing else but pease and pork, and boiled beef".[2] Approaching England, the restored monarch had begun the tale of his escape after the Battle of Worcester; his frequent repetition of which was later to bore his courtiers to politely dissembled agonies. In Pepys he had a feeling listener: "It made me ready to weep to hear the stories that he told of his difficulties that he had passed through."[3] Pepys rowed ashore ahead of the king, taking with him "a dog that the king loved". In the boat the dog behaved with the immodest abandon characteristic of dogs. Pepys innocently records his surprise that "a king and all that belong to him are just as others are".[4]

Upon landing, the king was received by the mayor of Dover, who presented him with a Bible. The king, accepting it, "said that it was the thing he loved above all things in the world".[5] A canopy was provided for him to stand under, "which he did", but not for long, before starting his progress to London. Pepys remained in Dover until 8 June, when he set out for London in charge of the king's guitar.[6] At Gravesend he kissed a good handsome wench, "the first that I had seen for a great while". That was still customary on greeting a woman, Pepys taking full advantage of the practice. On the king's way, writes Pepys, "the country gentlewomen did hold up their heads to be kissed by the king, not taking his hand to kiss, as they should do".[7] The king entered London on 29 May, his thirtieth birthday. A procession led by three hundred horsemen displayed the whole strength of what was left of Cromwell's army. He was received by both Houses of Parliament at Whitehall Palace. A service of thanksgiving had been arranged at Westminster Abbey, but the king was too tired to attend it, withdrawing instead, it was rumoured, to the sleek arms of Barbara Palmer, soon to become Duchess of Cleveland.[8]

Four months after Charles II's arrival, in spite of his promises of clemency, the executions began. "A bloody week this and the last have been", wrote Pepys on 20 October.[9] Even his rank appetite for spectacles was daunted. A military dictatorship having been replaced by an unprincipled despotism, Charles II was to prove as faithless to his loyalists as he did to his Parliaments, which he was in the habit of proroguing as soon as they had voted him money. One by one he betrayed, out of lazy indifference, the former Cavaliers, just as in the past he had betrayed Montrose. By the nature of its legislature, the society which Charles II brought into being was necessarily corrupt.

That was later seen. But on the night of the king's return to London, only the most rigorous Presbyterians absented themselves from the bonfires, the displays of fireworks, the fountains running wine. Mince-pies, plum-porridge and custard had been restored to the English nation.[10] In Oxford, Anthony Wood reports, everyone was putting up, though May was nearly over, the maypoles which had been prohibited under Cromwell. Busily and heartily the balked remnants of Puritanism were dispersed in *Hudibras*. Pepys bought *Hudibras*, when it first appeared in 1662, for 2s. 6d. but thought it so silly that he sold it to Mr. Townsend on the same day for 1s. 6d.[11] A month or two later he had to buy a second copy because everyone was talking about it: "It being certainly some ill-humour to be so against that which all the world cried up to the example of wit."[12]

Under the Commonwealth, the state's intrusions upon the privacy of the individual, which Milton had sarcastically postulated whilst writing against the censorship of books in *Areopagitica*, were actually brought about by his own party.[13] No music was indeed heard but what was grave and Doric. On 10 May, 1650, an Act was passed making adultery a capital offence, and fornication an offence punishable with three months' imprisonment; though there were few successful prosecutions, juries being unwilling to convict, in view of the harsh penalties entailed. One woman was bound over in the sum of £80 "to be of good behaviour for one year".[14] Nathaniel Nash, a soldier, being found drunk in the arms of Janet Ferris at Leith, both were sentenced at a court-martial to be ducked twice in Leith Harbour.[15] On 16 May, 1650, an Act was published for the better observance of the Sabbath. Soldiers were empowered to enter private houses in London to ensure that the Sabbath was not being profaned; and also to prevent the monthly fast, which was decreed for the last Monday in each month, from being broken. Every kind of sport and recreation on the Sabbath was made a penal offence. Three boys were tried at Rye in 1654 for sliding on the ice.[16] On 7 June, 1650, a Bill was introduced to prevent women from painting their faces, wearing false beauty-spots and buying immodest dresses; but it was found to be unrealistic, and never received a second reading.[17] On 28 June, 1650, a scale of fines was fixed for cursing and swearing.[18] Above the rank of baronet the profane curser had to pay 30s. for the first offence. A gentleman paid 6s. 8d. and an inferior person 3s. 4d. A wife or widow was fined according to the rank of her husband. In default of the fine, the offender was put in the stocks if over the age of twelve or, if under, whipped. The theatres were closed, the maypoles cut down, dancing, boxing and cudgel-play discountenanced. Horseracing and wrestling were placed under an interdict. The number of ale-houses ("where drunkenness is sold and harboured", according to Milton's *Areopagitica*) was reduced.[19] The English people were subjected to the tedium of a defined existence. No swearing, no dancing, no drinking, no theatres, no horseracing, no sliding on the ice, no fornication: there was hardly anything for them to do. The violence of the reaction against Puritanism at the Restoration of Charles II was due to the fact that for fourteen years the Puritans had bored, beyond the possibility of further endurance, those not of their way of thinking.

Whilst it would be too much to say that it was a mark of one's loyalty to the crown to fornicate, commit adultery and swear as much as possible, it did at least prove that one was on the right side. Certainly great changes took place in what was deemed acceptable conduct. The Earl of Rochester, a thirteen-year-old undergraduate at Oxford, previously noted for the tenacity of his classical studies, promptly gave them up at the Restoration, frequenting the taverns instead in a borrowed Master's gown; and so inaugurated the years of debauch which ensured his death at the age of thirty-three. Though the king contrived an absolute government, though he nonchalantly renewed ceremonial hanging as the penalty for High Treason, witnessing four of the executions himself, his careless people gave themselves to tumult and excess. London became a licentious capital. Rochester said that the devil entered him whenever he came to Brentford on the way to London, and never left him till he returned to the country.[20] With some indignation Pepys relates how the drunken poet Sir Charles Sedley, writer of weak pastoral gallantries and father of one of the Duke of York's mistresses, had to be bound over, on a surety of £5,000, for heedlessly relieving himself from a balcony in Covent Garden, then giving a blasphemous explanation to the startled crowd that assembled.[21] In his satire, *A Ramble in St. James's Park*, Rochester disapprobated the lewd trees of that fashionable quarter; indicating that all sorts of abandoned behaviour took place beneath their shade.[22] Milton sternly surveys the streets of Restoration London in *Paradise Lost*, published in 1667:

> where the noyse
> Of riot ascends above their loftiest Towrs,
> And injury, and outrage: and when Night
> Darkens the Streets, then wander forth the Sons
> Of Belial, flown with insolence and wine.[23]

Some patriotic historians have averred that the court of Charles II learned dissolute habits during the long exile in France, returning to vitiate a blameless England. In fact, French manners during the minority of Louis XIV were particularly decorous and formal. Encapsulated by the court of Louis XIV, the former Cavaliers there preserved, in all their solemnity and authenticity, the conventions of the circle of Charles I. Restoration England was just the bawdy old England of Jacobean times getting going again with an initial violence. The frequent improprieties of the most characteristic literary form of the Restoration, its comedy, were by no means borrowed from the French. Although many plots and some characters were taken from Molière, Molière himself is one of the chastest of authors. The comic dramatists of the Restoration merely resumed the manner and the idiom of Ben Jonson, Thomas Middleton and John Fletcher.[24] The plays of Etherege and Wycherley, for example, are perfectly in the tradition of Middleton's comedies, *A Chaste Maid in Cheapside* and *The Roaring Girl*. The citizens continue to hunt down the gallants' patrimonies; the gallants continue to hunt down the citizens' wives. In the manner of Jonson, such lesser dramatists as Shadwell relied for the most part on the comical effect of consistent, predictable characters in whom one peculiarity curiously predominates. For some years Jacobean plays held the stage in the reopened theatres. Even when enough time had passed for the comedies of the Restoration itself to be written and produced, the innovations were theatrical rather than dramatic. Sir William Davenant, as playwright and impresario, introduced scenery on the stage, and the dramatists luxuriated in the possibilities this gave rise to.[25] In *The Fairy Queen* of 1692 two swans turned themselves into fairies and danced a measure, a sonata played whilst Phoebus rose, the stage was illuminated with the prospect of a Chinese garden, and Juno appeared in a machine drawn by peacocks.[26]

Shadwell sets one scene of his *True Widow* in a theatre, where two of the characters are carried up in their chairs, and hang in the air until they are let down by the stage carpenter. A third character is drawn up on a rope by a devil. For no reason at all except a love of spectacle, Sir Credulous Easy rode in on the back of an elephant to serenade his lady in Aphra Behn's *Sir Patient Fancy* of 1678.[27] Davenant also introduced actresses, who often appeared out of their skirts, so inducing lascivious raptures in Samuel Pepys. On 28 October, 1661, he recorded that he went to the theatre, "where a woman acted Parthenia, and came afterwards on the stage in men's clothes, and had the best legs that ever I saw, and I was very well pleased with it".[28] By February, 1663, he was setting up as a connoisseur. He went to see *The Slighted Maid*: "Though the play hath little good in it, being most pleased to see the little girl dance in boy's apparel, she having very fine legs, only bends in the hams, as I perceive all women do."[29] All five of the female characters in Aphra Behn's *The Feigned Courtesans* of 1679 dress up as young men at some stage of the plot. This was true to an age when the Earl of Rochester, practising in the City as a German physician and astrologer, was visited there by the Duchess of York's maids-of-honour disguised as orange-girls.

Two theatres were licensed in London: at Drury Lane, under the king's protection, and at Lincoln's Inn, under the Duke of York's. Performances were usually in the afternoon. Pepys sometimes went to the theatre twice in one day. The audience was drawn mainly from the aristocracy and its hangers-on. Old-fashioned citizens avoided the theatre as disreputable, which it often was. The actors became so drunk during the performance of one play that it had to be abandoned after the third act.[30] During an early performance of *The Relapse*, the actor playing Worthy, utterly befuddled, went so far beyond his role as to attempt to violate the heroine.[31]

Charles II loved the theatre so much that he once lent his coronation suit to the actor Betterton for a part in one of Davenant's plays.[32] To Dryden he suggested the plot of *Secret Love*, and to Crowne pointed out the original of *Sir Courtly Nice*.[33] At his instance Otway introduced the satire on Shaftesbury in *Venice Preserved*.[34] Thus the theatre, like every other institution in Restoration England, spun on the shaky hub of a Baroque kingship. The king directly intervened in the course of the drama, persuading Lee, Otway and Dryden to write rhymed tragedies in the French manner, and sending Betterton to France to study the French stage.[35] Lee's *Mithridates*, a tragedy in the French mode, was rewarded with an amateur performance at court; the future Queen Anne in the part of Semandra.[36] The monarch was like that Margrave of Baden who, in the early eighteenth century, built Karlsruhe so that the belvedere surmounting his palace was the exact centre of the town, all the streets and all the avenues of his park either irradiating from it or concentric with it. From his belvedere the margrave could contemplate the stars and the streets alternately, certain that he was the axis of the Universe of Karlsruhe. The dominance of the court was one reason why public interest waned during the reign of James II, when the king was found uncongenial, and the prestige of courtly institutions diminished with the ebbing of loyalty from him.

Vested though it was in the tainted kingship, cruel and untrue, of Charles II, pledged though it was to the outward deportment of his court, the comedy of the Restoration inherited the concerns of comedy in all times: the absurdities and follies of mankind; departures from a silently affirmed propriety. Comedy is the art of smiling censure: censure which entails assessment and the sense of moral law. To this effect wrote the Earl of Roscommon, in the free translation of Horace's *Art of Poetry* which he published in 1680:

> Poets, the first instructors of mankind,
> Brought all things to their proper native use;
> Some they appropriated to the Gods,
> And some to publick, some to private ends;
> Promiscuous love by marriage was restrained,
> Cities were built, and useful laws were made;
> So great was the divinity of verse,
> And such reverence to a Poet paid [37]

To the same effect wrote Aphra Behn in her verses on Creech's translation of Lucretius:

> But as of old, when Men unthinking lay,
> E'er gods were worshipped, or e'er Laws were framed,
> The wiser Bard that taught them first t'obey,
> Was next to what he taught adored and famed;
> Gentler they grew, their Words and Manners changed;
> And savage now no more the Woods they ranged.

The prologue of Etherege's *The Man of Mode* points out that the follies of the public provide the material for the comic dramatist:

> For, heaven be thanked, 'tis not so wise an Age
> But your own Follies may supply the Stage . . .
> 'Tis by your Follies that we Players thrive,
> As the Physicians by Diseases live. [38]

The epilogue, written for Etherege by Dryden, asserts that the satire in *The Man of Mode* is not personal, but general. Sir Fopling Flutter represents the collective follies of the audience:

> Yet none Sir *Fopling* Him, or Him, can call;
> He's Knight o' th' Shire, and represents ye all [39]

There must be a consonance between dramatist and audience in their notions of a moral law, otherwise the action of the play will be found not comic but pointless, or even reprehensible. The dramatist is not the song of the wind but the branches it blows through. It is not the honest and the faithful who are censured in Restoration Comedy. A comic dramatist can speak to his public only in a common language of assumptions concerning the decencies. Although the age may neglect those decencies, the dramatist in representing the neglect cannot condone it. In a comedy, whatever action is performed is inevitably a comment on actions of that sort; such is the purpose of comedy. What deals only with the oddities of persons is not comedy but farce.[40] Thus a distinction must be made between the often licentious stories which are told in Restoration Comedy and the ultimate moral earnestness with which they are told. The play should not be judged before the play is done. In a Restoration comedy everyone receives his deserts except the hero and the heroine, who sometimes receive better than their deserts; though being married to each other might be regarded as punishment enough for some of them.

It must be admitted that in the Prologue to *The Royal Shepherdess* of 1669 Thomas Shadwell laments the absence of a system of rewards for virtue and punishments for vice in the comedies which he as much as anyone was writing at the time:

> It is a Vertuous Play, you will confess,
> Where Vicious men meet their deserv'd success.
> Not like our Modern ones, where still we find,
> Poets are onely to the Ruffians kind;
> And give them still the Ladies in the Play,
> But, 'faith, their Ladies are as bad as they.[41]

But not even Shadwell, except in the sanctimonious *Royal Shepherdess*, operates a facile system of rewards and punishments. Like Wycherley, a more ferocious moralist than he, Shadwell sees that his characters receive what they deserve by letting them establish for themselves the convention by which they are treated by other people. A man who is a wolf to other men is likely to be treated as one. At the end of Shadwell's play *A True Widow*, Gartrude the female waster is obliged to marry the male waster Young Maggot, author of "An Epigram written in a lady's bible at church", and other works. Young Maggot believes her to be an heiress. By a savage moral twist Shadwell leaves the newly wed Maggot learning that Gartrude has no fortune at all; whilst Gartrude makes an assignation on the spot with one of her former lovers.

Equally sardonically, Wycherley's *Love in a Wood* ends in the failure of Dapperwit, the duping dupe, and of all the other tricked tricksters. Dapperwit is cheated into a disadvantageous marriage with an heiress who has shed both her honour and her fortune. Those who have made insincerity their way of life are consequently treated with insincerity. Those who have lived by the sword die by the sword. Mistress Loveit in Etherege's *The Man of Mode*, who lived by the flesh, dies by the flesh. "Fairest isle", sang Dryden in his *King Arthur* of 1691:

> Fairest Isle, all Isles Excelling,
> Seat of Pleasures, and of Loves;
> *Venus* here will chuse her Dwelling,
> And forsake her *Cyprian* groves.

> *Cupid,* from his Fav'rite Nation,
> Care and Envy will Remove;
> Jealousie that poysens Passion,
> And despair that dies for love.

> Gentle Murmurs, sweet Complaining,
> Sighs that blow the Fire of Love;
> Soft Repulses, kind Disdaining,
> Shall be all the Pains you prove[42]

So sang Dryden retrospectively, with a graceful hedonism which was quite out of date in 1691. Dryden was growing old. The moral tale of the Earl of Rochester suggests that the England of Charles II was more like Baudelaire's Cythera than Dryden's.[43]

Shameless, pushful, militant for an all-too-permitted freedom, without humility, maturity of judgement, experience of the world or any but the rawest and most imitative notions of conduct, Rochester designated himself a law unto himself in the London of 1665. He belonged to a fellowship aggressively, and perhaps luckily, bent on the destruction of its members. Their sexuality was the cosy, accommodating sexuality, though a trifle smeared, of the pigsty and the monkey-house. A systematic disordering of all sentiments and all decencies took place, and as a physical by-product of that modish degeneration an epidemic of syphilis broke out. This Rochester caught. Unwiser than the unwise steward, Rochester used his talent to purchase Death. Sternly he exercised his inalienable right to debase himself and his abilities. Later he told Bishop Burnet that he was continuously drunk for five years.[44] Nothing illustrates the collapse of order and institutions in Restoration England better than the way in which Rochester was smilingly allowed to obscure and then obliterate his inherent glory. The true villains of *Romeo and Juliet* were the nurse and the friar.

There was an early Christian sect which sought to attain purity by the ritualistic practice of debauch; and it is possible that it is only through a tired satiation, such as is so often depicted in the comedy of the age of Charles II, that a state of absolute purity, in volition as in act, can be reached. The intention declared by Charles Baudelaire in composing *Les Fleurs du Mal* was to prove, by a prolonged exploration of vice, that it is less enjoyable than virtue. "Ce misérable dictionnaire", he wrote in the original dedication to Théophile Gautier, "this miserable dictionary of melancholy and crime can justify the responses of morality, just as blasphemy is evidence in favour of belief." He concludes *Un Voyage à Cythère* with the words:

Ah! Seigneur! donnez-moi la force et le courage
De contempler mon cœur et mon corps sans dégoût!

Rochester's evidence is the more persuasive in that, unlike Baudelaire, he had no avowed purpose in his investigation of a brutal carnality.

On 19 June, 1680, he called his family and servants together, and read them a document expressing his abhorrence of his past life. This he afterwards signed.[45] The next day his friend

William Fanshaw visited him, to be urged by Rochester to repent of his former life and amend it. "There is a God," he said, "a powerful God, and he is a terrible God to unrepenting sinners."[46] Thus the consequences of Rochester's choice, disregarded at the moment of choice, were exalted into the fancy of a punishing God; as if a choice does not imply a responsibility. Fanshaw could find nothing to say, but only stole from the room, warning the people of the house to keep Rochester from such melancholy fancies. One has the sense that the whole of Restoration England was flying from that grim sickroom.

Yet the lesson which the Earl of Rochester so painfully taught had already been inculcated by a dozen Restoration comedies. The comic dramatists reflected their audience's manners, which were urbane, nonchalant and free-spoken; but went on to assume a priestly or vatic function and act as informal judges of their audience's conduct. Since comedy moves always in the direction of the eternal decencies, the unity of Restoration Comedy with its age was only such as one cloud appears to have with another when it traverses it. But the topics which recur in Restoration Comedy are those in which the age was naturally and endlessly interested: the education of a gentleman, the value of honour in a man and chastity in a woman, the respective merits of tradition and innovation, the contention between constant and inconstant love, the trials and penalties of marriage in a loose-living society, the promoting of felicity and the avoiding of sorrow.

Three years before the death of Rochester, Aphra Behn had published, in her *Town Fop*, a scene which illustrates, not Rochester's first view but his last. "To an exact perfection", wrote Rochester:

> To an exact Perfection they have brought
> The action Love; the passion is forgot.[47]

What desperation, what disillusion with physical love, lies underneath the mannered depravity of Aphra Behn's hero in his encounter with the whores:

(Enter Flauntit, Driver, Doll and Jenny masked.)

BELLMOUR. Oh damn 'em! What shall I do? Yet it would look like Virtue to avoid 'em. No, I must venture on—Ladies, y'are welcome. . . .

SIR TIMOTHY. Come, come, approach her; for if you'll have a Miss, this has all the good Qualities of one—go, go Court her, thou art so bashful—

BELLMOUR. I cannot frame my tongue to so much Blasphemy, as 'tis to say kind things to her—I'll try my Heart, though— Fair Lady—damn her, she is not fair—nor sweet—nor good— nor—something I must say for a beginning. . . . Gods! What an odious thing mere Coupling is! A thing which every sensual Animal can do as well as we.[48]

In a way, Aphra Behn has preached a powerful sermon here. If this is her own estimation of promiscuity, no wonder she loved to surround it, in her plays, with glossy and attention-consuming intrigues.

Though Lord Macaulay calls *The Country Wife* "one of the most heartless and profligate of human productions", throughout his plays, and especially in *The Country Wife*, William Wycherley shows himself to be a severe moralist; as his friend, Lord Lansdowne, said, "Not adorned for parade but for execution".[49] *The Country Wife* illustrates a Christian principle: that vice lies in the volition as well as the action. A play almost merry in the exuberance of its fervent mistrust of human nature, *The Country Wife* weights falseness against truth. Horner deludes others, Pinchwife deludes himself. Mrs. Pinchwife pursues into the desert of disrepute the mirage of pleasure. Horner pretends that he has been surgically emasculated so that he can approach in peace and woo other men's wives: including Pinchwife's country girl, whom Pinchwife has married believing that her ignorance of vice will keep her from it. The husbands of the play, relying on Horner's supposed inability to make love, are not concerned with the moral purity of their wives, but only on the physical fact which is incidental to it. Pinchwife relies on his bride's unawareness of vice, not her reasoned dislike of it. As Sir Richard Steele wrote in an account of an eighteenth-century production of the play:

"There is no defence against vice, but the contempt of it."[50]

The comic dramatists of the Restoration were not bent on the advancement of adultery. If they had been, few people would be amused. The spectacle of two deceivers abusing a trusting third person can only be repugnant. But to protest against the tricking of Pinchwife in that special situation is as absurd as to say that Lady Wishfort is ill-treated in *The Way of the World* or Lady Cockwood in *She Would if She Could*. It is a question of intent. Pinchwife's marriage did not take place with the girl's consent, but only that of her parents. There is no tenderness on his part:

> MRS. PINCHWIFE. Oh my dear, dear Bud, welcome home; why doest looks so fropish, who has nanger'd thee?
> PINCHWIFE. You're a Fool.
> (*Mrs. Pinchwife goes aside and cries.*)[51]

He threatens to kill her squirrel if she misbehaves. It is precisely because he thinks her a fool, not because he thinks her inherently chaste, that he marries her, confident that she will never have the cleverness to deceive him; so he can hardly complain when she behaves foolishly rather than chastely. Horner provides the cleverness.

In *The Country Wife* Wycherley presents a world of appearances, a hall of mirrors shining into each other, deterring the beholder's eye from penetration by flashing back at him the similitude of his own opinions and prejudices. In *The Plain Dealer* Manly puts his sea-boot through a few of the mirrors and finds: emptiness, vacancy. The discoverer in *The Country Wife* is Pinchwife himself, but Wycherley despises him for the docility with which, knowing himself to be deceived, he continues to warm himself in the luxury of the deception:

> For my own sake fain I wou'd all believe;
> Cuckolds, like Lovers, shou'd themselves deceive.
> (*He sighs.*)[52]

With the other men Horner keeps up a semblance of friendship,

cuckolding some, fooling them all. Their friendship is recip-
rocally false. "Though I have known thee a great while,"
Sparkish says to Harcourt, "never go, if I do not love thee
as well as a new Acquaintance."[53] When Horner's friends hear
about his sad loss, they are vastly amused, and make him the
butt of their cruel pleasantries, though this is nothing to the
butt he makes of them. By resuming his disreputable friends
when he returns from the country, by thinking he can apply
a double standard, keeping his wife chaste whilst he reverts
to his old dissolute life himself, Pinchwife to some extent
brings about his own misfortunes. "Marriage-frauds too oft
are paid for in kind", and Pinchwife's friends are all too willing
to help in that repayment.[54]

Wycherley's close friend Dryden calls *The Plain Dealer* a
"superlatively bold and useful satire".[55] Indeed, Manly's
opening speech is like the confident onset of one of Rameau's
harpsichord pieces, the confidence in every way justified by
the brilliance of the variations that follow:

> Tell me not (my good Lord Plausible) of your Decorums, super-
> cilious forms, and slavish Ceremonies; your little Tricks, which
> you the Spaniels of the World, do daily over and over, for, and
> to one another; not out of love or duty, but your servile fear.[56]

Wycherley gives the plot an additional satirical twist by making
his misanthrope's judgement weak. Although Manly's low
view of humanity is perhaps justified by most of the characters
of the play, it is the faithful minority whom he most fails to
trust: his friend Freeman and the game little Fidelia.

However one turns over the many original documents which
exist about Wycherley, one comes no nearer to discovering the
true man. Always conscious of the fronts and subterfuges of
others, Wycherley in turn reveals little except his manners,
which are elegant ones. He was found to be urbane, a little
ponderous, somewhat untalkative: "Slow Wycherley", Rochester called him.[57] He gave little away about himself. That he was
a passionate man one may guess from many passages in his
plays, but he seems to have cultivated a Hobbesian suppression

of the feelings. His youth had taught him to endure and to be self-sufficient; but it was a lonely endurance and a self-sufficiency without joy. Was there ever a play so loveless as *The Country Wife*? Was there ever a promise of love more specious than that between Manly and Fidelia in *The Plain Dealer*? Wycherley may have felt himself to have been separated in some way from human love. The composed outwardness of his life was perhaps sustained by a total unsureness about how the slightest discomposure would be received. At his very heart there was an equivocation: a contempt for artifice and an understanding of its usefulness. The tragic cry of his nature (during his disastrous marriage to the Countess of Drogheda; during his imprisonment in the Fleet Prison) was unvoiced, dwindling into a sigh hastily stifled. In his play, *The Gentleman Dancing Master*, his hero Gerrard, posing as a dancing master, though ignorant of the business, and though infuriated by his own pretence, is forced to give a lesson before two critical witnesses. People looked to Wycherley as a dramatist to set the fashion; as a kind of dancing-master to guide their movements in the artificial performances of society. Well, then, he leads them on, none too sure of the steps himself, but lamenting and raging, at least, to a defined rhythm.

Whilst Wycherley's dissent from his society was masked by a carefully simulated indifference, Rochester's in his late satires was outright and clamorous. The first set of his satires were still comparatively equable, although *A Letter from the Town to the Country* is a satire on the prostitution of love by fashionable promiscuity. Here Rochester militates against himself and his own earlier standards. In the character of Corinna, Rochester represents the self-betrayals of a woman who followed the libertine mode as he had followed it himself. The poem, *On Charles II*, which shades over into the ferocious moral satires, has a gloss of bonhomie upon it which does not really conceal its contempt.

There are three intensely felt moral satires by Rochester: *A Satire on Mankind*, *A Ramble in St. James's Park* (which Professor Sola Pinto rightly calls a powerful and indecent poem), and the unfinished poem generally known as *Roches-ter's Farewell*. They are in many ways like the later poetry of Charles Baudelaire: the fact that they are not quite sane does not detract from their moral earnest. They have the force of Jeremiah inveighing against Jerusalem, of Juvenal pounding at the city of Rome with piled-up loathing, of Dante prowling the lurid cinders of the Inferno. Rochester was a Pharisee who had chosen to live in Babylon. With the violence and preci-pitousness of the puritanism latent in him, Rochester pours down the apocalyptic brimstone of his indignation upon the new city of the plain: on sentiments cheapened into the drill of physical stimulation; on love becoming at its best a neuras-thenic exercise; on Nell Gwynne following strange practices to revive the flagging virility of the king; on the Duchess of Mazarin parading awash with the attentions of a succession of admirers; on the indiscriminate welter beneath the trees in the purlieus of the court.

Lucretius, whom Rochester admired and translated, asserts that the only Hell is the one that fools make for themselves on earth. Rochester had made his Hell, but he was not far wrong in supposing that it was the Hell of his age:

> To an exact Perfection have they brought
> The action Love; the passion is forgot.

What discovery can Charles II have made on that night in 1685 when, amid his mistresses who were the common property of his court, he fell forward on the card-table piled with his people's gold, his face blackening? What thoughts sustained him on his death-bed, before he sent for the priest? The memory of what accomplishments shone before his eyes? In the *Satire on Mankind* it becomes clear that the moral satires are externalised self-hatred, Rochester's savage wiping-out of his own front lines:

> But Man with smiles, embraces, Friendships, praise,
> Inhumanely his Fellows life betrays.[58]

Rochester met his earlier self like a stranger. But with a stranger we are faced not only with a conformation, but with the history of a conformation. The nature of every identity is that of a record of the past. Alien though the young Rochester was to the older Rochester, there could be no expunging of the still activating past:

> Slowly the poison the whole bloodstream fills.
> It is not the effort nor the failure tires.
> The waste remains, the waste remains and kills.[59]

There was to be no escape from having been Rochester. This was the harmatia, and the silent nemesis. He "blazed out his youth and health".[60] As in a holly sapling set on fire, the flames shot up through the kindling greenwood. Rochester has often been compared, in his failed idealism, to Milton's Satan; and certainly the devil was, after all, a fallen angel. Great ill-doers have so much in common with saints because both functions require a sacrifice of ease and moderation; and it is the common, cautious and expedient practice of a vice which is damnable. Yet in Rochester's later poetry there is less defiance than regret. The image of a collapsed archangel is too Byronic. Byron was vain but not self-centred. His aim was always, by display and dominance, to project himself. Rochester, on the contrary, was self-centred. His concern was a resolution of his inner life. The right image for him and for his generation is less heroic and more tragic than any to be found in *Paradise Lost*. It is in the *Odyssey*, where Homer describes the pigs in Circe's sty, weeping over their memory of Ithaca.

CHAPTER TWO

The Sons of Belial

THE TERM, RESTORATION LITERATURE, is generally used of a tradition diffused beyond the strict historical limits of the Restoration itself. Only the earlier comic dramatists, of whom the most important are Etherege, Shadwell, Mrs. Behn and Wycherley, wrote during the reigns of Charles II and James II. The members of the second generation, which included Congreve, Vanbrugh and Farquhar, wrote nothing before the reign of William and Mary. Dryden deployed himself over both generations, publishing his first play in 1664 and, with a strong sense of the appropriate, not dying until 1700. With these seven Sons of Belial—and one daughter—we shall begin.

1. Sir George Etherege, c.1635–1691

Sir George Etherege was born into the Berkshire squirearchy but never speaks of the country without distaste.[1] We first catch sight of him at one of the Inns of Court, where, having apparently spent part of his youth in France, he was sneeringly, and only at the request of his father, studying municipal law: "a fair slender genteel man but spoiled his countenance with drinking", according to one of his contemporaries.[2] Like his own Sir Frederick Frollick, he was sometimes a party to brawls, once at least in the company of his friend, the Earl of Rochester. They were at Epsom, tossing some fiddlers in a blanket for refusing to play, and a barber coming to see what the matter was, they seized him too. To free himself from them, he offered to take them to the handsomest woman in Epsom, but in fact meanly directed them to the constable's house. When the constable asked them what they came for, they told him, "A whore", and so he refused to let them come in. At that they broke down the door and beat him until he escaped to fetch the watch. Here Etherege brought into play his powers of persuasion, which must have been remarkable. He made "a submissive oration to them and so far appeased them that the constable dismissed the watch". Later the brutal farce turned into a tragedy, and a man was killed; but by that time Rochester and Etherege had run away.[3]

From 1668 to 1670 he was Secretary to the Ambassador at Istanbul, and was praised for the shrewd observations he made in his dispatches on the characters of the people he met there.[4] Charles II knighted him in about 1680, perhaps to help him marry the elderly heiress who became his wife at this time.[5] Etherege soon stopped living with her, and altogether fled her in 1685, when James II appointed him Ambassador in Ratisbon (now called Regensburg), the diplomatic capital of the German Empire, at the excellent salary, for those times, of £3 a day plus expenses.[6] Seldom was a more disreputable ambassador sent abroad; or one with a less deserved reputation as a judge of character, since he failed to notice that his own Secretary, who was sending home malicious secret reports on Etherege, virulently disliked him. At The Hague, wrote the Secretary, Etherege lost £250 at play, haunted pitiful and mean houses, and was "sufficiently laughed at" for his love-making; and from The Hague to Ratisbon he caressed "every dirty drab that came in his way".[7] Etherege did not trouble to pay any formal diplomatic calls until he had been in Ratisbon for several months. Instead, he and his drunken companions used to parade the streets of Ratisbon "with clubs in their hands to guard themselves and their music. . . . The town could never be rid of them till cold weather began to keep them at home."[8]

Etherege's three comedies had been written in an overflow of energy during his busiest years. During the long idleness at Ratisbon, and indeed during the last fifteen years of his life, he wrote hardly anything. He was dejected by the quietness of Ratisbon and the formality of an ambassador's life. In a letter to Lord Sunderland he owned that, in spite of all his efforts to enliven it, Ratisbon remained a dull town. He was forced to sit at home and "entertain himself with solitude and silence". For want of knowing what to do with himself he went to bed at night. He feared that his regular hours would endanger his health. It was as if the Diet had passed an imperial decree against the pleasures of play and women. For a while Etherege had been cheered by the company of the Countess of Nostitz, "but malice that always persecutes the good had made her lately remove to Prague".[9] Etherege consoled himself by taking into his care a young actress from Nuremberg; so adding to the uproar he had already caused. Naturally, it did not make the most decorous of effects when the British Ambassador's carriage waited all night long, and most of the next day, outside an actress's lodgings; "for fear", suggested Etherege's secretary, "that the town should not come to the knowledge of the scandal". Leaving the theatre, he sometimes put the actress publicly in his coach "notwithstanding all the giggling and hishing of the Austrian ladies", himself humbly returning to the Embassy on foot.[10] This unusual Ambassador's release from Ratisbon came sooner than he had thought. At the beginning of 1689 James II was deposed. With relief and perhaps embarrassing loyalty Etherege flew to the king's side in Paris, where he died two years later.

2. Thomas Shadwell, 1641–1692

Thomas Shadwell, a Norfolk man of sound armigerous family, was educated at Caius College, Cambridge, and the Inner Temple.[11] He made most of his income from writing plays, and married an actress, Anne Gibbs, who *created* the part of Emilia in his *Sullen Lovers*. During the reign of James II he was in disfavour for his blunt Whig and Protestant opinions, but at the Glorious Revolution he was made Poet Laureate in place of the non-juring Dryden. His well-known quarrel with Dryden had taken place in 1682, at the time of the Bill to exclude James II from the throne. Shadwell was the aggressor. In the first part of *Absalom and Achitophel* and *The Medal* Dryden had attacked Shadwell's party and its leader, the Earl of Shaftesbury. In 1682 Shadwell replied with the personal lampoon, *The Medal of John Bayes* (John Bayes being a nickname for Dryden), in which he accuses Dryden of sexual perversion and of having written a panegyric on Cromwell. Dryden, not a forgiving man, at once retaliated with *MacFlecknoe*, and for good measure inserted an even more insulting description of Shadwell in the second part of *Absalom and Achitophel*, which was otherwise written by Nahum Tate. Dryden's satire on Shadwell in *Absalom and Achitophel* is not of the most delicate kind. He calls him "a monstrous mass of foul corrupted matter" and advises readers to stop their noses at the mention of his name.[12] Shadwell brought this active year of 1682 to a close with two further satires on Dryden. In *The Satire to His Muse* Shadwell calls Dryden's wife "a rank whore" who had two illegitimate children and a miscarriage before Dryden was bullied into marrying her.[13] In *The Tory Poets* he charges Dryden with having invented hitherto unknown vices, and repeats his slanders on Dryden's wife. Here the dispute ended until 1689, when Shadwell wrote a satire on Dryden's conversion to the Roman faith.[14] Between them Dryden and Shadwell created a small literature of abuse which does credit to neither of them. Shadwell wrote most and had the last word; but Dryden's contribution was the deadly and memorable one.

Shadwell is said to have taken opium "to raise his imagination".[15] If this is true, there is little evidence that the opium was effective. It is also claimed that Shadwell helped his country's economy greatly by the large sums he spent in customs duty on his claret.[16] He was a prosaic and unflowing writer, but sharp-eyed and full of homely rationality and humour. His coarse, well-meaning face may be studied on his monument in Poet's Corner in Westminster Abbey. If Etherege deserves the epithet of "easy", Shadwell deserves that of "uneasy". His dialogue is often forced and unchiming, with dragged-in modish slang and dialect. Observant but unsubtle, he seldom contrived a fluent interchange. In some ways he reminds one of Dickens, and would indeed have been happier as a realistic novelist. In his lists of parts he gives character sketches more suitable for a novel:

Colonel Hackwell, an old Anabaptist colonel of Cromwell's, very stout and godly but somewhat immoral.

Mrs. Jilt, a silly affected whore that pretends to be in love with most men, and thinks most men in love with her, and is always boasting of love-letters and men's favours.

Sir Timothy Kastril, an ugly sub-beau, but has a mortal hatred to war, that leads a lazy dronish coxcombly life, writing billets-doux.

Mrs. Woodly, jilting, unquiet, troublesome and very whorish.[17]

Excluded from the circle of court dramatists because of his Whig politics, Shadwell went his own way to a large extent. A parish Ibsen in a scratch-wig, Shadwell is notable for his sustained interest in social issues. Starting as a mere conciliator of public taste, he gradually reduced the knockabout content of his rough comedies (although he never eliminated it) and enlarged the discussion of the problems of the day, in a manner more familiar in the theatre of the early twentieth century. In his choice of hero, by a similar progression he replaced the man of mode with the man of honour, moving from the courtly ideal of the early Restoration towards the religiously based ideal of the eighteenth century. The prototype of Sir Roger De Coverley and Sir Charles Grandison already existed—in Etherege's *The Comical Revenge* and elsewhere—but it was Shadwell who gave it pre-eminence; sacrificing some humour but gaining in exemplary effect. In this respect he revealed the strength of the levitical tendencies which he shared with those other middle-class moralists, Addison and Richardson.

3. Aphra Behn, c.1640–1689

According to the earliest biography of Aphra Behn, written by one of her friends, she was born, the daughter of a gentleman of Canterbury called Johnson, during the reign of Charles I.[18] She may have been in the West Indies from 1658 to 1660.[19] In 1665 she appears to have been briefly married to a Dutchman called Behn. The forced marriages and the marriages to

B

old men which are recurring features in her plays may have been based on her own experience. She next went to Antwerp as a spy, a heavyweight Mata Hari in the Low Countries, but failed to obtain her salary from Charles II, for whom she was endangering her life. She returned to London in 1667, sick and badly in debt.[20] Here she formed an irregular attachment to John Hoyle, a lawyer of Gray's Inn. He was a freethinker and an admirer of Lucretius.[21] To judge from the catalogue printed for the sale of his library in 1692, he was something of a scholar. Apart from the mere hundred law-books, the library contained over a thousand volumes, many of them choice and costly works in Latin, with copious marginalia by Hoyle himself.[22] Unfortunately for Aphra Behn, he had little inclination for women. According to contemporary scandal, his taste lay in another direction.[23] He seems to have treated Aphra Behn unkindly. On him as much as on the character of Dorimant in Etherege's *The Man of Mode* she probably modelled one or two vicious heroes in her plays.

Her first play, *The Forced Marriage*, appeared in 1670. As a result she made the acquaintance of Waller, Dryden and Rochester. She was popular with the young wits, and they with her. A zealous Tory, she was imprisoned in 1682 for a slight on the Duke of Monmouth.[24] But she remained firmly Protestant, and was outraged when Dryden became a Roman Catholic.[25] Attacked for her unwomanly aspirations, she defended herself in a preface of 1686: "I value Fame as much as if I had been born a Hero".[26] Constantly worried by debt, she did certainly struggle like a hero. The first woman known to have earned her living solely as an author, Aphra Behn wrote sixteen plays (as well as a number of novels, poems and translations) in nineteen years; dying, apparently of rheumatic fever, in 1689.[27] She was one of the most unexpected people to be buried in Westminster Abbey, where her tombstone may still be seen in the cloisters.

There is something a little chilly about many of her comedies. She was a woman of great intelligence, and capable of poetic intensity, especially if compared with the prosaic Shadwell. In her plays there is an underlying melancholy. At their most sombre they contain a desperate glacial cynicism which out-does anything the male dramatists were capable of. The devoted submissive letters which she is supposed to have written to John Hoyle hardly suggest a Scarlet Woman, nor do her features in the portrait by Sir Peter Lely: her prominent forehead, pudgy nose and abstracted frown.[28] It is as if she was vying with the men to prove that a woman could succeed wherever they did, could have as few illusions and be as heartlessly witty. Whilst Etherege's satire is affable and gener-ous, and Shadwell's has a rustic forthrightness, that of Mrs. Behn is often sour and watchful.

Her plots are full of improbabilities: of disguises, mistaken identities, misdelivered assignations, and confused skirmishes in the dark. All five female characters in her *The Feigned Courtesans* at some point dress up as young men. Of the male characters, three appear in disguise, and the identity of the fourth is concealed from the others. The Italian courier Petro grows rich on English travellers by appearing, in rapid succes-sion, as a barber, a Jewish broker, a fencing master, a dancing master and an antiquary, all recommended by each other. Plots are not Aphra Behn's chief merit, though her stage-devices created some exuberant theatrical spectacles. Where she does excel is in cynical grace and cadence of expression, ludi-crous invention and witty incident.

In her later years she wrote several short novels. They have an arresting ejaculatory style, and the openings immediately capture an attention which unfortunately the narrations do not retain. Her use of plausible detail may well have influenced the novels of Defoe; but her story-telling is garrulous and over-circumstantial. She runs on uncontainably and tediously. In her poems, in which she represents herself as enslaved to a succession of Amyntases, Strephons, Alexises and Lycidases, there are occasional pangs of sincerity, but much allusion to flowery beds, soft charms, oaten pipes, jocund swains and nymphs transported with delight; though mockingly enumer-ated. Love's sacred flame is tended, souls melt, and there is amorous strife. The poems are mostly wan and sapless pastorals, February eclogues, faded like an old tapestry, wafting in Aphra Behn's soft limpid drone. They are all love poems. Her *Pilgrim's Progress* was a Voyage to the Isle of Love.

In *The Feigned Courtesans* Mr. Galliard describes the apartment of the supposed Silvianetta: "All's wondrous rich, gay as the court of Love, but still and silent as the Shades of Death".[29] The description could well be used of the plays of Aphra Behn. She wrote comedies with a breaking heart; labouring away in a mood of breezy disillusion. Her comedies often depict the downfall of a dissolute woman, and such a dark moral comedy is her own life. Full-sailed, Baroque and gracious, her ship drops beneath the horizon, returning from the Isle of Love, with what depths of bitterness under the timbers!

4. William Wycherley, 1640–1716

William Wycherley was the eldest son of a Royalist gentleman of Shropshire who was forever engaged in lawsuits against his neighbours. Wycherley may well have been portraying his father, with a change of sex, in the character of the widow Blackacre in *The Plain Dealer*: "Her Lawyers, Attornies and Solicitors have Fifteen hundred pounds a Year, whilst she is contented to be poor, to make other People so."[30] The terrible Daniel Wycherley is even said to have imprisoned his own son, William Wycherley's younger brother, for debt.[31] With an all-providing absolutism Old Wycherley put William through the rudiments of Latin, flogging it into him, until he spoke Latin like an Ancient Roman. At least this tyrannical education fixed in Wycherley's mind the idioms and rhythms of Augustan poetry, so that in his own style there is something of the curt, clipped effectiveness of Horace.

At the age of fifteen Wycherley was sent to France to round out his studies. Old Wycherley was determined that the heir to Clive Manor should not receive his education from a pack of Roundheads. In France Wycherley came under the influence of the Marquise de Rambouillet, the forty-year-old leader of the group of learned women known as "Les Précieuses", and later satirised by Molière in his comedies, *Les Précieuses Ridicules* and *Les Femmes Savantes*.[32] Their bluestocking salons testify to the social and cultural power of the women of the French aristocracy, which had continued since the time of the medieval courts of love. But instead of *contestations d'amour* the seventeenth-century *tribunaux* adjudged questions of Greek and Chemistry. The marquise, a friend of Voiture, Corneille and Richelieu, was forever getting up amateur theatricals, conversaziones and ballets. The Précieuses had two sides. They encouraged young writers, promoted many useful schemes of research, and by their enterprise and ingenuity fostered an intellectual excellence; but, having a sense of accomplishments which were unusual in their sex, and being assertively anxious to display them, they fell into habits of vainglory and affectation. Wycherley presents both sides of the Précieuses in his younger female characters. Perhaps all his heroines he based on some aspect of the marquise, just as Richardson is said to have based both Mr. B. and Lovelace on different aspects of the Duke of Wharton. They were in general dashing and sprightly-minded, good managers and contrivers, with a gay confidence in their own abilities; but, like Olivia in Wycherley's *The Plain Dealer*, capricious, pretentious and affected.

Wycherley was educated in the ways of the world by the Marquise de Rambouillet. As Lord Chesterfield advised his son, it is very educative for a young man to spend his time with an older woman of fashion. More, being among these brilliant people so much older than he, he learned how to smile and hold his tongue, which accentuated the secretiveness he always showed about his own opinions and feelings. But he did not spend all his time at the Château d'Angoulême playing charades and intellectual parlour games. He also contrived to be received into the Roman Catholic Church; an instance of moral earnest but one which gave no great pleasure to Old Wycherley when Wiliam returned to England in 1660, a few weeks ahead of the king. Old Wycherley saw to it that William was swiftly reconverted, sending him to Queen's

College, Oxford, where his friend, the well-known theologian Thomas Barlow, was Provost. Wycherley lodged in the Provost's quarters.[33] It could hardly have been agreeable for a vigorous young man of twenty to lodge with the head of his college, especially when the Provost was corresponding with his father. Wycherley followed no regular course of studies, and got out as soon as he could, without troubling to take a degree. He persuaded his father that he would be more useful if he studied law in the Inner Temple in London, so that he could help with the many family lawsuits.[34] Wycherley's six months at Oxford left him with no reverence for academic life. In *The Country Wife* he makes Sparkish say: "This is Ned Harcourt of Cambridge, by the World, you see he has a sneaking Colledge look."[35]

Wycherley spent the next twelve years doing as little as possible, just observing the town and not coming much further in the study of law. Like Manly in *The Plain Dealer*, Wycherley was briefly engaged in the sea-fight against the Dutch in 1665. Dorset and Rochester were present on the same occasion. They went off in their fringed gloves and their tasselled pantaloons to cannonade the shopkeeping Dutch. Rochester behaved with audacity, although he may have been drunk at the time. Dorset wrote a famous poem, *To All You Ladies Now on the Land*, on board his ship. Wycherley wrote a less famous poem, *To a Jilting Mistress Ashore*, which gives a hint of Olivia's behaviour to Manly in *The Plain Dealer*.[36] When he became James II, the Lord High Admiral remembered Wycherley, and helped to release him from a debtors' prison in 1686.[37]

Love in a Wood, Wycherley's first play, was produced in 1671 and published with a dedication to Barbara Palmer, Duchess of Cleveland, in the following year. Wycherley's language throughout the play is that of Charles II's court, though heightened and pointed by Wycherley's own plain terseness. His love of maxims emerges in such shrewd phrases as: "The jealous, like the Drunkard, has his Punishment with his Offence."[38] Wycherley's style, like that of Aubrey Beardsley's drawings, lies partly in the discretion with which superfluous detail is eliminated. The part of the hero, Ranger, was played by Charles Hart, a former lover of the Duchess of Cleveland. She came to an early performance of the play, wearing the famous pearls which had cost Charles II £40,000; and went home thoughtful. The next day her carriage happened to collide with Wycherley's in Hyde Park. She leaned over to him and called him a name which Lord Macaulay primly says could more justly have been applied to her own children.[39] Wycherley, always civil, made a gallant reply, which must have been hard to think of, and obtained permission to call on her the next morning. So it was that Wycherley came to share a mistress with Charles II; and not with Charles II only. Barbara Palmer was thirty and still beautiful. Lely painted her portrait at this time, as the goddess Bellona, and it still hangs at Hampton Court. She is wearing armour and big ear-rings. But when she came to visit Wycherley at his lodgings, she dressed as a working girl, in clogs and a straw hat.

Such was the charm of Wycherley's conversation, and so gentlemanly his air, that the sight of his lank, loose, sarcastic face pleased all companies. In his old age, said Pope, he had "the nobleman look".[40] But Wycherley was retrospectively vain of his appearance in his youth. He chose for the frontispiece of his poems, published when he was sixty-four, an engraving of Lely's portrait painted when he was twenty-eight.[41] Under it he had printed in Latin: "How he has changed!" The amour with Barbara Palmer nearly brought upon Wycherley the enmity of her cousin, the Duke of Buckingham, who had long but ineffectually wooed her, but Wycherley's grace and accomplishments captivated Buckingham too; so that at the end of an evening they had spent together as the guests of the Earl of Rochester, Buckingham cried out, "By God, my cousin is in the right."[42] Because Wycherley was such a wit, Buckingham, now his staunch friend, appointed him Captain of the Household Cavalry.[43] Charles II was not jealous of the new encroachment. He was at that time more interested in Frances Stewart and, with his aloof, undemanding sensuality, was quite glad that Barbara Palmer had a distraction; so he welcomed Wycherley to the small club of her lovers, invited him to private parties, and occasionally gave him a hundred pounds. In 1677, when Wycherley lay sick of a fever, Charles II visited his lodgings, sat down by his bed, and gave him money to convalesce in the South of France.[44]

Wycherley did not marry until he was thirty-nine. His late marriage, and the absence in the many contemporary memoirs which mention him of any reference to his love affairs, apart from the brief and worldly one with the Duchess of Cleveland, suggest some obscure coldness in his nature. In 1679, having voiced so much wariness and circumspection about marriage in his plays, he made the worst possible marriage himself, to the slatternly and sinister Countess of Drogheda, whom he met whilst they were both taking the waters at Tunbridge Wells. It is hard to know why he married her, unless touched by the crazy abandon of her passion for him. She had driven a former husband first mad and then to his death; and she was now disastrously in debt.[45] The kindest thing one can say about her is that she was probably not very sane herself. To Wycherley she was a lurid Fury who brought him as a dowry bankruptcy and a legion of self-perpetuating lawsuits. Charles II, disapproving of the marriage, withdrew a proposal he had made that Wycherley should tutor his illegitimate son, the Duke of Richmond, at a salary of £1,500.[46] Wycherley and the Countess settled into Wycherley's old lodging in Bow Street. When Wycherley went to the Cock Tavern across the road the raging countess insisted that the windows there should be left open so that she could see that he was not talking to any women.[47] It may have been fortunate for Wycherley that the countess soon died; but as a result of her debts, and the extravagances of the marriage, he spent the next seven years in prison for debt.

The conditions at Newgate Prison would have discouraged a man less stoical. Though only a debtor, Wycherley, used to the hand-shake of a king and the arms of a king's mistress, wore leg-irons.[48] Just as in his marriage, not a groan, not a single confidence, rose to his lips. The only comment he made, in a letter to a friend, was a grim jest about how quickly he lost his new acquaintances as they were taken off to be hanged.[49] Instead of execrating his lot, he stolidly formed and executed a plan to be transferred to a new prison. The Fleet was bad enough, but at least it was better than Newgate. Charles II, offended at Wycherley's marriage and loyalty to the fallen Duke of Buckingham, spitefully ignored his plight. Wycherley was eventually rescued, and pensioned too, by James II. There were not many kind actions in that sour life, so let us make the most of this one. Just as Wycherley lost the goodwill of Charles for his loyalty to Buckingham, so he lost his pension at the Glorious Revolution for his loyalty to James II. He retired to the country, which he abhorred, not returning to London until the death of his father. Upon his return he settled into a life of comfortable dissipation on the income of the entailed estate he had inherited; much admired as an ancient monument by all, and especially by Alexander Pope, who dedicated one of his *Pastorals* to him.[50]

Wycherley's last play, *The Plain Dealer*, had been published in 1677. Now, after a lapse of twenty-seven years, he resumed his literary life. In 1704, at the age of sixty-four, he published his *Miscellany Poems*. Versification was not Wycherley's talent, and the poems have all the suave grace of a baby elephant. Their chief interest is that Pope corrected some and stole from others. Wycherley chooses unconventional and surprising subjects at all costs, and gives his poems garrulous titles: *To a Fine Young Lady, Who Being Asked by Her Lover Why She Kept Such a Filthy Thing as a Snake in Her Bosom, Answered 'Twas to Keep a Filthier Thing Out of It, His Hand*, or *Upon a Lady's Fall Over a Style by Which She Showed Her Backside, Which Was Her Best Side*. He wrote two long poems on the last subject, which clearly entertained him greatly. There is a foolish elderly wickedness, not capable of much harm, in the poems. At the age of seventy-five Wycherley remarried, and died ten days later, perhaps from his matrimonial ardours.[51]

Wycherley was the last of the first generation of the comic

dramatists of the Restoration. The new generation started with William Congreve. Congreve did not fail to praise his fiercer predecessor. In the Prologue to *Love for Love* Congreve, modestly disregarding his own first two plays, wrote:

> Since *The Plain-Dealer*'s Scenes of Manly Rage
> Not one has dar'd to lash this Crying Age

The amiable and gracious compliment to the worth of an elder comrade was characteristic of Congreve. Congreve was, in fact, in Wycherley's debt. In Congreve's *The Old Bachelor* Heartwell derives from Wycherley's Manly (although Wycherley shares his character's misanthropy whilst Congreve does not) and Fondlewife inherits the misfortune and some of the mannerisms of Wycherley's Pinchwife.

5. *William Congreve, 1670–1729*

It was now the reign of William and Mary. No longer the predatory Stuarts slunk through St. James's Park in a dark pituitary flush. The seraglio lay open to the sky, the concubines were dispersed. Rochester was dead, Etherege in exile. Wycherley had retired into Shropshire. In London Aphra Behn lay sick. An austere, asthmatical Dutchman and his gentle bluestocking wife now shared the throne and set the nation an example of domestic composure. In her patchwork closet Queen Mary sat with her maids of honour, mending tapestries for the royal couple's Baroque and marbled extension to Hampton Court Palace. Over English society William and Mary diffused an air of decorum and serenity. A little because of this, more because of the even, measured wit of Congreve, the drama became less ribald, more seemly and temperate. Humorous eccentricity of the Jonsonian sort lost ground (partly, too, because of the increasing influence of the ladies) to scandal, repartee and social intrigue.

William Congreve was born near Leeds in 1670. Like Etherege and Wycherley, he was born into a Cavalier family and like them studied the law without much diligence in the

Temple. The Temple was a good look-out post from which both ends of the town, the court and the city, could be observed. Congreve's father moved to Ireland during Congreve's infancy, to command a garrison there, and Congreve went to school in Kilkenny.[52] Here he early showed his charm and talent by writing an elegy, which has unfortunately not survived, on the death of his master's magpie.[53] From Kilkenny Congreve went to Trinity College, Dublin, where he was a fellow-student of Jonathan Swift.[54]

Congreve's first work, a short novel called *Incognita*, was published in 1691. He prefaced it with a sententious distinction between a romance and a novel, in which he points out that he has copied dramatic techniques, and confined the action to the space of three days. *Incognita* is in a tradition established by the novels of Mrs. Behn, and in spite of the grave declarations in the preface is a preposterous narrative of masks, disguises, a dropped handkerchief, a letter written and then torn up, love and duty reconciled, and predestined lovers. As one would guess from the fastidious tunefulness of his syntax, Congreve delighted in music. During his early years in London he was much taken by the singer and lutanist Arabella Hunt, and published a poem about her in 1692. He describes something like the sensation Keats felt when listening to the nightingale. The sense of peace in these lines, the liquefaction of quietness, is general in Congreve's verse. Almost as soon as he arrived in London, Congreve won the regard of the elder man-of-letters, Dryden, who came to regard Congreve as his literary heir. For Dryden's *Juvenal*, also published in 1692, Congreve translated the Eleventh Satire. Congreve's translations from the classics have a moderated wildness, like a Bacchante in repose on a Wedgwood teapot. Whilst Pope's classicism is superimposed on his work, that of Congreve runs through all his being like the stripe through an agate. It is the Halicarnassos Frieze in Meissen china instead of marble, the contours the same, but with delicacy replacing strength. The resonant individuality of his prose style lies partly in his constant, slightly withheld approximation to the idioms and rhythms of Latin. The language of Millamant owes as much to Juvenal as it does to the prattle of the fine ladies of the Restoration.

In 1693 Congreve's first play, *The Old Bachelor*, edited for the stage by Dryden, was performed. It ran for a fortnight: unusually long for those days. It was equally successful as a book, three editions appearing in as many months. The heroine was played by Anne Bracegirdle, the most famous actress of the age. She *created* the part of the heroine in each of Congreve's plays, including that of Millamant, and in each of his plays Congreve delayed her entrance till the second act, so that it should make a stronger effect. From the loose actresses of the Restoration stage, with their slippery accessible thighs, Anne Bracegirdle was set apart by her celebrated chastity, from which she deviated, legend says, only in favour of Congreve, by whom she may have had a child.[55] She probably acted characters in Congreve's plays based on herself in the first place. She was seven years older than Congreve, who was twenty-three when *The Old Bachelor* was produced: surprisingly young to have written such a worldly and knowledgeable play. Even so, he said that he wrote it several years before it was first acted, to amuse himself "in a slow recovery from a fit of sickness".[56]

Later in 1693 Congreve's second comedy, *The Double Dealer*, was produced. Although it was not a failure, it did not enjoy the absolute public success demanded by the rigorous Congreve, who became angry with the public as a result. He preferred *The Double Dealer* to *The Old Bachelor*, and was shocked that the second play did not earn the applause given to the first.[57] The plot of *The Double Dealer*, like that of *The Way of The World*, is over-complicated. There is a string of eccentric types, as in the plays of Shadwell: Froth, a solemn coxcomb, Brisk, a pert coxcomb, and so on. Congreve tried to re-establish some of the features of the Jacobean stage, such as the soliloquies and the intricate Machiavellian betrayals. His villain, Maskwell, is a kind of polite Iago. The audience had only the faintest enthusiasm for such devices when used in a comedy, and the play had little luck until Queen Mary, paying one of her rare visits to the theatre, attended its second run, and was so pleased with it that she commanded a revival of *The Old Bachelor*, which she had not yet seen. For that Congreve wrote a special prologue saying that she should come to the theatre oftener.

Moderate though the public's zeal for *The Double Dealer* had been, the play won Congreve compliments from two of the best judges of the time, Dryden and Swift. Dryden, in a verse preface to the published version, officially designated Congreve his successor:

> Be kind to my Remains; and oh defend,
> Against your Judgment, your departed Friend!
> Let not th' insulting Foe my Fame pursue;
> But shade those Lawrels which descend to You.

Fairy godparents surrounded Congreve's literary infancy. A steady drift of offices of state, none of them with more than nominal duties, settled upon William Congreve.[58] In 1695 he became a commissioner for the licensing of hackney coaches, in 1705 a commissioner for wine licences, and in 1714 Secretary for Jamaica, an island he was content to administer from his house in Surrey Street, just off the Strand.[59] There was a general conspiracy to be kind to Mr. Congreve. Even when the government fell, the unwritten law was observed: all else might change, but Mr. Congreve must continue to license hackney coaches. Under Whigs and under Tories he licensed them with careless impartiality, becoming expert at the task. In his moments of relaxation from his public cares he had the pleasure of hearing himself extolled by almost every considerable writer living in London at the time.[60] It was well that Congreve had these consolations of worldly advancement and praise, since his own body played him false. Gradually he went blind: cataracts thickened over a crystalline vision. As if that was not enough for a lonely scholar to bear, he became crippled too, from gout. The more for his afflictions, he liked to lose himself in his lifelong devotion to music.

His patroness, Queen Mary, died in 1695. Exquisitely, with sensitive modulations of regret, he lamented her in an eclogue—

a Hampton Court pastoral called *The Mourning Muse of Alexis*.
Dr. Johnson describes *The Mourning Muse* as "a despicable
effusion of elegiac pastoral; a composition in which all is
unnatural, and yet nothing is new".[61] It is no more unnatural
than a Brandenburg Concerto or a madrigal by John Dow-
land. In its delicate ornamentation it is an apt requiem for
a queen who delighted in embroideries and grave formal
gardens. *The Mourning Muse* conveys a sense of a landscaped
garden, such as Rousham near Oxford, of the early eighteenth
century. The neat domestic bees wing in, laden with their
sticky, faintly odoriferous loot. The lead statues of nymphs
and agrarian deities seem in motion in the vibrant evening
haze. The grotto and the carefully ruined temple crown the
perspective. Now that Queen Mary, called Pastora, is dead,
the sheep feed again who, in her lifetime, could never stop
gazing and begin grazing. Tears run down the cold marble
of her vault. The light which made her eyes brilliant mounts
into the sky:

> The Fawns forsake the Woods, the Nymphs the Grove,
> And round the Plain in sad Distractions rove;
> In prickly Brakes their tender Limbs they tear,
> And leave on Thorns their Locks of Golden Hair.[62]

No doubt this is artificial, but no more so than *Comus* or *Lycidas*
or the Bucolics of Virgil himself. At any rate, William of
Orange was highly pleased and, whether he actually read the
elegy or not, sent Congreve £100 in thanks.[63]

In 1695 the actor Thomas Betterton broke away from the
Theatre Royal in Drury Lane, taking with him several of the
best members of the company, and built a new theatre on a
tennis court in Lincoln's Inn Fields. Congreve was offered a
share of the profits on condition that he wrote exclusively
for the new theatre, and he agreed, if his health permitted,
to write one play for it every year. The new theatre opened with
Love for Love, which he had completed in 1694.[64] *Love for Love*
is by far the longest of his plays, and in it he celebrates his
ever-increasing attachment to music by including three songs,

as well as dances. It contains many good things, but its interest is too dispersed in subsidiary considerations. The raw, Shadwell-like characterisation of Ben Legend and Mr. Foresight, the endless nautical jargon and astrological gabble, is tiresome; yet in the same year as *Love for Love* Congreve published *A Letter concerning Humour in Comedy*, in which he confesses a dissatisfaction with such characters based on the Jonsonian humours. *Love for Love* lives chiefly for Mr. Tattle and Miss Prue.

For about two years Congreve subsided into the indolent melancholia which became habitual with him in his later life. He roused himself only to write from Tunbridge Wells complaining about the waters, which he calls "Anti-Hypocrene" : "I know not whether these Waters may have any Communication with Lethe."[65] Lethe is the river of Death as well as of forgetfulness. The portrait of Congreve by Kneller records a mane of loose blond peruke, a flinging air, and eyes sharply resolute in the mannered repose of the face. There is no trace in it of the recurrent depressive bouts, the tears shed in private, the inquietude beneath the airy cravat, the romantic despair of his lines in *The Mourning Bride*:

> There we will feast, and smile on past Distress,
> And hug, in scorn of it, our mutual Ruin.[66]

When Congreve re-appeared, it was with this tragedy, *The Mourning Bride*, which, though little known nowadays, was more popular in the theatre of his own time than any of his comedies. The play suggests the untidiness of Death to an ordered mind. Dramatically it is insipid, in spite of much bloodshed and such lines as "The eastern gate is to the foe betrayed" and "Bear to the dungeons those rebellious slaves". On the other hand, from the moment when the curtain rises, to soft music, there is a majestic sense of motion and rest, of alternate melody and quiet. The scene in the cathedral, which was such a favourite with Dr. Johnson, is replete with silence.[67]

Congreve now, in spite of his repugnance for such unmannerliness, was drawn into a public argument. A Jacobite parson called Jeremy Collier published in 1698 his hoarse and conceited *A Short View of the Immorality and Profanity of the English Stage*, a low and often silly work, verbose and in its way lewd, directed chiefly against Congreve and Vanbrugh. The reverend gentleman had evidently read many profane plays with great diligence. He accuses the playwrights of swearing and blasphemy: Lady Plyant in *The Double Dealer* "cries out Jesu and talks smut in the same sentence"; Congreve burlesques the Holy Scriptures by calling a coachman Jehu.[68] Collier quotes the law against swearing in big Gothic letters.[69] He deplores the disrespect with which the playwrights treat clergymen and persons of rank and fortune, such as Lord Foppington. He denounces the poor moral character of Freeman in *The Plain Dealer* and Valentine in *Love for Love*, and is shocked by their not coming to a bad end. He objects to Young Fashion's marrying Miss Hoyden in *The Relapse*, which he is unperceptive enough to call a reward.[70]

Collier made an effect out of all proportion to his size, starting a controversy which has rolled on into our own age. Macaulay, who shared Collier's views, for that reason exaggerated his importance, and spread a legend that Collier stepped forth like a headmaster quelling an unruly Third Form, and smartly brought the comedy of the Restoration to an end. That is not true. Vanbrugh and Congreve's replies to Collier were far from subdued. The fullest fruition of Restoration Comedy in *The Way of the World* was yet to come. None of the plays of Farquhar had yet been written. Restoration Comedy came to an end ten years later, partly because the possibilities of a limited convention had been exhausted; partly because Farquhar died, Congreve became blind and gouty, and Vanbrugh was engrossed in his architecture. These events had nothing to do with Jeremy Collier.

Amongst the replies to Collier which appeared, and the replies to the replies to replies, Vanbrugh's brisk *Vindication* of 1699 was the merriest contribution. He finds fault with Collier's moral character, supposing that it has been debauched by reading so many bawdy plays.[71] He sifts the full ridiculousness of Collier. The moral question, Vanbrugh points out, is distinct from that of earthly rewards. The characters in a play are not necessarily models of conduct. The spectator is encouraged to form his judgements from a heightened representation of life, in which people really do, deplorable though it may be, swear. "I'm ashamed", Vanbrugh provokingly says, "that a clergyman can spin his mischief no finer". Congreve at first found it more dignified to ignore Collier, but irritated that he might be supposed conscious of a deserved rebuke, he issued his *Amendments of Mr. Collier's False and Imperfect Citations* towards the end of 1698. Congreve's objection was a just and scholarly one: that Collier had no business to argue from quotations taken out of their context. But he was unable to reply so coolly as Vanbrugh. Congreve was the dramatist most roughly treated in *A Short View*. More sensitive than Vanbrugh, infuriated by Collier's presumption, and loathing the vulgarity of his prose-style, he wrote with anger and contempt, describing Collier's hands as very dirty.[72] "He teaches those vices he should correct, and writes more like a pimp than a priest. . . . His office requires him in another place than the theatre."[73] Collier's reproof is more licentious than the dramatists' practice. He racks "bawdry and obscenity out of modest and innocent expressions"; and having extorted it, he scourges it "not out of chastisement but wantonness".[74] In short, says Congreve, he even deserves to be something so regrettable as Jeremy Collier.[75] The indignation of Congreve's reply reveals his basic sensibility and emotionalism.

Breathing heavily, Congreve settled into the composition of *The Way of the World*, in which he places the *Short View* alongside the cherry-brandy in Lady Wishfort's closet. At thirty, before many others have started, Congreve completed his life's work as a dramatist. Already he was persecuted by the gout and spending his time at one spa after another. Light stung his eyes and he appeared nowhere without the brim of his hat drawn down over them. In March, 1700, he inaugurated the new century with the first performance of *The Way of the World*. The importance he attached to its composition and style is proved by its publication before the month was out. The play had no great success on the stage. The plot is more complicated even than is usual with Congreve. There is a great deal of off-stage intrigue and little action, though a profusion of witty incident. It was altogether too subtle for Congreve's public. As William Hazlitt observes, the force of style in this author at times amounts to poetry.[76] But the audience was not interested in the tender portrayal or Congreve's fastidious private outpourings at the altar of whoever was the original of Millamant. In his use of her Congreve reminds one of the calm with which the gods received the metamorphoses of their loves. Syrinx turned into a reed, so Pan played a tune on her. Bacchus grew tipsy on the grapes of the tendril-haired Ampelus.

During the remaining twenty-nine years of his life Congreve wrote little apart from some poems and a couple of short operas; one of which, *Semele*, was later set to music by Handel. He liked to be thought of as a gentleman rather than an author, and such time as he did not spend with the Duchess of Marlborough he gave to his health, his music and his dogs. All his life he had attracted ardent attachments to himself, and now, nearly crippled and nearly blind, the line of his august midriff loose and portly, he took possession of the mind of Henrietta Churchill, beautiful and far younger than Congreve; Duchess of Marlborough, daughter of the victor of Blenheim, daughter-in-law of Queen Anne's chief minister, the Earl of Godolphin, with whose son she lived on terms of friendly estrangement.

Congreve died from injuries he received, helpless as he was, when his coach overturned on the way home from Bath in the autumn of 1729.[77] The Duchess of Marlborough saw to it that Mr. Congreve's coffin was brought to his grave in Henry VII's Chapel by a duke, an earl, two peers, a brigadier and a colonel. There has been some criticism of Congreve for leaving the whole of his fortune of £10,000, as well as such personal possessions as his Library and his crested silver, to so rich a woman as the Duchess of Marlborough.[78] The facts are these. Congreve had spent the summer of 1722 with the Duchess of Marlborough at Bath, where he was noticed to be especially attentive to her.[79] In 1723 her daughter Mary Godolphin, the future Duchess of Leeds, was born. The Duchess of Marl-borough invested most of the money Congreve left her in a diamond necklace, which in her own will of 1733, first published in 1964, she left, with the remainder of Congreve's fortune intact, and all the personal relics, to Mary Godolphin.[80] One should not jump to conclusions. On the other hand, slighter evidence would be accepted in a divorce court.

Congreve had spent the last twenty years of his life immersed in the English aristocracy, like one of those small joyful creatures in the paintings of Hieronymus Bosch who unctuously enclose themselves in immense hollow fruits. He found his way around Godolphin House with the erect-headed and direct walk of the blind, seeking perhaps Henrietta's arms, a shelter of silky textures and evanescences. He was a relic of patrician ideals enshrined in a patrician reliquary. Henrietta's devotion to Congreve survived his death, and only ended with her own four years later. She used all her womanish expediency in contriving to be buried next to Congreve in Westminster Abbey, putting him next to the Godolphins' grave, and insist-ing that she should be buried with the Godolphins, instead of with the Churchills at Woodstock. One is touched, and reminded of Teresa Guiccioli's prostration of herself on Byron's grave-slab. The sleepy Francis Godolphin had himself buried in Kensington Church, leaving Congreve and Lady Henrietta alone at the Abbey.[81] He was an obliging husband to, and even after, the last. The quiet dust of that passion has lain there in the mingled grave for more than two hundred years.

6. Sir John Vanbrugh, 1664–1726

Sir John Vanbrugh wrote the draft of his second original play, *The Provoked Wife*, in the Bastille; surroundings not surprising for a man of such varied experience. Vanbrugh was born in 1664, one of the nineteen children of Giles van Brugg, a sugar-baker of Flemish descent living in Chester.[82] Vanbrugh did not want to become a pastry-cook like his father, and obtained a commission in a regiment of foot instead, accom-panying Marlborough to the war, and rising to the rank of captain. In 1690 he was arrested by the French on a charge of espionage, and in 1692 Louis XIV ordered him to be imprisoned in the Bastille, where he remained for nearly a year.[83] Life was dull but comfortable there. Vanbrugh was treated as one of the prisoners of quality, who were each allowed one bottle of Burgundy at lunch and two at dinner. So provided for, he diverted himself with his problematic discussion, in dramatic form, of female honour. At the end of 1692 Vanbrugh was exchanged for a prisoner taken by the English, and returned to London to resume his military career. He was still one of Marlborough's officers at the time when he wrote his first play, *The Relapse*.

The Provoked Wife, produced in 1697, though a theatrical success, excited scandal because of the scenes in which Sir John Brute ran wild—drinking, whoring and beating the watch—disguised as a parson. It was the immediate reason for Jeremy Collier's *Short View*. That eccentric and Jacobite clergyman, living in hiding on a charge of disaffection to the crown, was incensed by the disrespect shown to his cloth. He condemns Vanbrugh, amongst other things, for having blasphemously denied the Scriptures.[84] Had not Amanda, in *The Relapse*, controverted the Book of Genesis: "What slippery stuff are men composed of! Sure the account of creation's false, and 'twas the woman's rib they were formed of"? Vanbrugh at once answered Collier in his good-humoured *Short Vindication*. In it Vanbrugh affirms his moral purpose: "The Business of Comedy is to shew People what they should do, by representing them on the Stage, doing what they shou'd not".[85] But, encouraged by Collier, the Middlesex magistrates began a tentative prosecution against Betterton's company for performing *The Provoked Wife*. Queen Anne, on her accession four years later, settled the differences between the two sides by instituting the licensing of plays by one of the officials of her court. She also forbade women to attend the theatre in masks; and encouraged the building of a new and less profane theatre in the Haymarket. The new theatre, designed by Vanbrugh, was opened in 1705 as a house, managed by Vanbrugh and Congreve, for Betterton's company! The only effect on Vanbrugh of Collier's strictures was that in 1725, when *The Provoked Wife* was revived, he disguised Sir John Brute, not as a parson, but as Lady Brute; which was surely more offensive.

During the opening years of the new century Vanbrugh, more and more interested in architecture, was making the transition from his second to his third career. Between Collier's attack and the completion of the Queen's Theatre in the Haymarket he adapted three plays from the French and, in collaboration with Nicholas Hawksmoor, designed Castle Howard in Yorkshire. He bought the site in the Haymarket for £2,000 in 1703, and borrowed large sums of money to build on it.[86] It was the first of his vainglorious and impractical edifices. The theatre's empyrean roof floated on incredible aspiring columns. It was superb; and scarcely a word spoken on the stage could be distinctly heard. Vanbrugh's venture lasted less than a year. As a soldier he had been tiresomely put in the Bastille and was, furthermore, unable to obtain his arrears of pay.[87] As a playwright he had been gibed at by a low, non-juring clergyman and left with a monumental useless theatre on his hands. It was time for something new: he would design a palace for his old General, the Duke of Marlborough.

Castle Howard had gone on being built for so long that its owner, the Earl of Carlisle, lost interest in it and left it unfinished; but used his influence as First Lord of the Treasury to have Vanbrugh appointed as one of the royal architects.[88] In that capacity, and as a sound Whig, Vanbrugh was chosen to build Blenheim Palace, to the annoyance of the Duchess of Marlborough, who, disliking Vanbrugh's magniloquent style, would have preferred something on the lines of Wren's Marlborough House. Throughout the building of Blenheim she quarrelled endlessly with Vanbrugh, driving him to resign his commission there in 1716. Sarah Churchill was much plagued by Restoration dramatists, and conducted another notable quarrel with her daughter, Henrietta, over Henrietta's association with William Congreve.[89] Also by the favour of

Carlisle, Vanbrugh established a foothold in his fourth profession in 1703, when, although he was ignorant of heraldry and had indeed made fun of it in *Æsop*, he was appointed Clarenceaux King of Arms. In 1705 he must have been working at the same time as a playwright, impresario, theatre-manager, Comptroller of the Royal Works, private architect at Castle Howard, Surveyor for the building of Blenheim Palace and second-in-command at the College of Heralds. It is not surprising that this Cadet Roussel of the arts did not marry until he was fifty-four.

The house which Vanbrugh built for himself from the ruins of Whitehall Palace was so tiny that Swift, in one of his burlesques, described people as walking about looking for it, but not finding it because it was only five times the size of a mud-pie:

> Thrice happy poet! who mayst trail
> Thy house about thee like a snail.[90]

After that Vanbrugh's manner to Swift became "very civil and cold".[91] At least for the Duchess of Marlborough Vanbrugh built a roomy enough house, "a house but not a dwelling", as a contemporary called it.[92] The severest criticism came from Horace Walpole in 1761. It did not placate the owner of Strawberry Hill that Vanbrugh himself had once built a Gothick summer house at Shotover Park: "He seems to have hollowed quarries rather than to have built houses. . . . The laughers, his contemporaries, said that, having been confined in the Bastille, he had drawn his notion of building from that fortified dungeon".[93] Perhaps there was some truth in the supposition that the ponderous amplitudes of the Bastille, his whole environment for one impressionable year, haunted Vanbrugh's recollections. He himself lightly admitted: "One may find a great deal of Pleasure in building a Palace for another; when one shou'd find very little in living in't ones self."[94]

Vanbrugh was a member of the Kit Kat Club, that group of Whigs who did so much to ensure the Hanoverian succession, and to shape the literature and politics of the early eighteenth century. His architecture was designed for Whig lords weighing twenty stone. His plays are in the Whig tradition continued by Addison: moderate, good-humoured, urbane, seeking to correct gently by ridicule, and stressing the merits of restraint and good manners. As Clarenceaux King of Arms and a stalwart party-man, Vanbrugh visited Hanover in 1706 to invest the Elector with the Order of the Garter; and when the Elector became George I of England in 1716, Vanbrugh was the first man he knighted.[95]

At Christmas, 1718, Vanbrugh was at Castle Howard. He wrote to the Duke of Newcastle: "'Tis so bloody Cold, I have almost a mind to Marry to keep myself warm".[96] A month later he wrote to announce his marriage to Henrietta Yarborough, who was thirty years younger than he: "'Tis better however to make a Blunder towards the end of ones life, than at the beginning of it. But I hope all will be well. . . . Jacob [*Tonson*] will be frightened out of his Witts And his Religion too, when he hears I'm gone at last. . . . I was the last Man left, between him and Ruin."[97] Six months later Henrietta miscarried of a baby girl. "And so", Vanbrugh wrote, "the business is all to do over again." The second and third times were more successful. "I am now two Boys Strong in the Nursery", he wrote, "but am forbid getting any more this Season for fear of killing my Wife. A Reason; that in Kit Kat days, wou'd have been stronger for it, than against it: But let her live, for she's Special good, as far as I know of the Matter."[98] Vanbrugh's marriage was certainly not like Sir John Brute's, and remained heretically happy until his death at the age of sixty-two, in 1726.

7. *George Farquhar, 1678–1707*

In many ways it is sad that Restoration Comedy comes to an end in the decidedly un-Herculean figure of George Farquhar. If we throw a rose away whilst it still has its scent, we remember it as a scented rose. It is a sere rose, only lingeringly fragrant, that Farquhar extends to us. His characterisation is slight, his first six comedies (though well contrived) embody no comment on the general nature of human experience, and he is only moderately funny. Here is Lady Lurewell, in his second play, *The Constant Couple*, informing the audience that she is a femme fatale:

> But now glance Eyes, plot Brain, dissemble Face, lye tongue, and be a second Eve to tempt, seduce and damn the treacherous kind—Let me survey my captives.[99]

And here is Colonel Standard, in the same play, being a man of honour:

> STANDARD. This only last request I make, that no Title recommended a Fool, Office introduce a Knave, nor a Coat a Coward to my place in your Affections; so farewell my Country, and adieu my Love! *Exit.*
> LUREWELL. Now the Devil take thee for being so honourable.[100]

Farquhar, a stage-struck undergraduate who became an actor himself, embarrasses his comedies with the monstrous rhetoric and the facile sentiment of the heroic plays of his time. Of all the comic dramatists of the Restoration, he is the most stagey. His early plays were written, with every success, to delight simple hearts.

George Farquhar was born in Londonderry in 1678, the son of a clergyman. Such events as the Siege of Derry and the Battle of the Boyne coloured his Ulster boyhood; which may be the reason why his plays are full of red-coated officers marching about their amours. One is constantly aware in his plays of Marlborough's army away at the front. During his last years at school Farquhar wrote an ode on the fall of General Schomberg at the Battle of the Boyne, which, like Farquhar's later verse, is without any distinction whatever. The third stanza opens:

> Gods! How he stood,
> All terrible in Bloud.[101]

In 1694 Farquhar became an undergraduate of Trinity

College, Dublin, but in the servile capacity of a sizar, who had to wait on the fellows and the richer undergraduates. This wretched experience seems to have made him socially unsure and assertive for the rest of his life. In *The Beaux' Stratagem* two friends and equals take it in turn to wait on each other as part of a ruse. The exacting studies at Trinity College, with formal instruction from 6 a.m. to 4 p.m., and the examinations four times a year, had helped to form the minds of Congreve and Swift. Farquhar was more interested in the Dublin theatre, and was repeatedly in trouble for town-haunting, brawling and even blasphemy.[102] In 1696 he finally ran away from the university and became an actor with the Dublin company.

The first part he played was that of Othello, an unnerving assignment for a beginner, and one which was clearly too much for him, since in the next Shakespearian production (*Macbeth*) he was given the role of Lennox, a Scottish lord. His career as an actor came to an end the following year, when by accident he severely wounded a fellow-actor whilst fighting a duel in an heroic tragedy. Farquhar was so horrified by the incident that he at once abandoned the stage. He came to London, where his first play, *Love and a Bottle*, was produced at the end of 1698. *Love and a Bottle* is a composition, both in its dialogue and in its plot, of borrowings from earlier Restoration plays; though the hero is an Irish gentleman newly arrived in London, and defensive about being Irish. The play was only moderately successful. It was Farquhar's second play, *The Constant Couple*, produced in 1699, which made his name.

Largely because the character of Sir Harry Wildair caught the fancy of the town, *The Constant Couple* enjoyed what was for that time the extraordinary run of over fifty days. Whilst *The Constant Couple* had this success at Drury Lane, *The Way of the World* failed at the new theatre at Lincoln's Inn; which is a good example of the frailties of popular taste. The public left Millamant and Mirabell to perish, and ran to acclaim Sir Harry Wildair. Boastful in his success, Farquhar wrote for the published version of the play, in 1700, a preface which suggests what a lightweight personality he had:

> I am very willing to acknowledge the Beauties of this Play. . . . I cannot call this an ill Play, since the town has allowed it such success. . . . Some may think (my Acquaintance in the Town being too slender to make a Party for the Play) that the Success must be derived from the pure Merits of the cause.[103]

Here he modestly adds that this is not his own opinion, in spite of what others may say. He continues:

> I have not displeased the Ladies, nor offended the Clergy; both of which are now pleased to say, that a Comedy may be diverting without Smut or Profaneness. Next to these advantages, the Beauties of action gave the greatest life to the Play .[104]

Such self-praise is not the result of confidence in great powers, but of parvenu anxiety. In his third play, *Sir Harry Wildair*, produced in 1701, Farquhar made the most of the principal character of *The Constant Couple*, to which *Sir Harry Wildair* is a sequel. It did not not in fact please the public as much as the original play had.

Farquhar, at the age of twenty-nine, was dying of tuberculosis when he wrote that merry work, his eighth and last play, *The Beaux' Stratagem*. Robert Wilks, the actor who had *created* the part of Sir Harry Wildair, not having seen Farquhar for two months, went to seek him out.[105] He found Farquhar helpless in a back garret in St. Martin's Lane, seriously ill, separated from his wife, penniless, and writing an epic poem on the Battle of Barcelona. Foolishly, he had sold his commission, preferring the immediate cash to the regular income. Wilks advised Farquhar to write a new play as quickly as possible. Farquhar replied that he had completely lost heart, and was too distracted by financial worries to write anything that made sense. Wilks gave him twenty guineas, told him to banish melancholy, and arranged to call again in a week's time to see the plan of the new comedy. In this way Farquhar came to write *The Beaux' Stratagem*, generally agreed to be his best and raciest play. He completed it in six weeks, writing most of it in bed in, as Wilks said, "a settled sickness". During the rehearsal of the play, Farquhar remarked, "My

life will be of shorter duration than the run of this play." The
first night was in March, 1707. In the pathetic, whimsical
epilogue Farquhar pleaded:

> If to our Play your Judgment can't be kind,
> Let its expiring author pity find.
> Survey his mournful Case with melting Eyes,
> Nor let the Bard be damned before he dies;
> Forbear you Fair on his last Scene to frown,
> But his true Exit with a Plaudit Crown;
> Then shall the dying Poet cease to Fear
> The dreadful Knell, while your Applause he hears.[106]

At the end of the following month Farquhar died, *The Beaux'
Stratagem* having done so well on the stage that *The Constant
Couple* had been revived too. Farquhar wrote a note to Wilks,
asking him to be kind to his two small daughters:

> Dear Bob, I have not anything to leave thee to perpetuate my
> Memory but two helpless Girls; look upon them sometimes,
> and think of him that was to the last Moment of his life, Thine, G.
> Farquhar.[107]

The last thing he wrote was a couplet, the sincerity of which
transcends its failure as poetry:

> Death now appears to seize my latest Breath,
> But all my Miseries will end in Death.[108]

He was buried, at the expense of Robert Wilks, in St. Martin's-
in-the-Fields, near the grave of Nell Gwynne, and with him
in Gibbs's rococo church was interred the comedy of the
Restoration.

CHAPTER THREE

Mode and Honour

THE COMEDY OF the Restoration was an aristocratic form which embodied aristocratic assumptions about the nature of eminence. Eminence is derived from the possession of wit, literacy and worldly grace, and subject only to the fierce and inexorable requirements of Honour. There is no reverence for the possession of money. The dexterity with which a man succeeds without it is often a qualification for eminence: certainly for Congreve's heroes Valentine and Mirabell. The bailiff's officers who attempt to arrest Valentine for debt say that they have half a dozen other gentlemen to arrest in the fashionable quarters of Pall Mall and Covent Garden. Congreve's heroes have no interest in money. They cede it to such as Mr. Fondlewife, who leaves his wife to the blandishments of her lover whilst he goes out to get £100: satisfaction less tangible than the plump cushion of Laetitia Fondlewife. An indefinite credit is all they require.

Something like the Hindu gradation of the castes operates. Highest come the wits and scholars; next the soldiers and administrators. The rich merchants and men of business barely come third. There is a contrast here with the comedies, for instance, of Sheridan. In Sheridan's comedies the assumptions are not aristocratic but plutocratic. The marks of social distinction have been put on a regular cash basis. In Sheridan's time, as his contemporary, Smollett, complains in *Humphry Clinker*:

> Clerks and factors from the East Indies, loaded with the spoil of plundered provinces; planters, negro-drivers, and hucksters, from our American plantations, enriched they know not how; agents, commissaries, and contractors, who have fattened, in two successive wars, on the blood of the nation; usurers, brokers and

jobbers of every kind; men of low birth and no breeding, have found themselves suddenly translated into a state of affluence unknown to former ages; and no wonder that their brains should be intoxicated with pride, vanity and presumption.[1]

The authority of Sir Anthony Absolute and Sir Oliver Surface rests upon their disposal of money. It was one of the effects of the Whig supremacy that the owners of riches were seen as the special instruments of Divine Providence. Another effect, due to the inherited puritanism of the city merchants, was an at least outward respect for religious obligations. Hearing a visitor coming upstairs, Lydia Languish tells her maid to hide the novels borrowed from the circulating library and leave Fordyce's *Sermons* open on the table:

> LUCY. O burn it, ma'am! The hairdresser has torn away as far as *Proper Pride*.
> LYDIA. Never mind—open at *Sobriety*.[2]

Millamant in *The Way of the World* curls her hair with the love-poems sent her by her dilettante admirers; Lydia Languish must make do with Fordyce's *Sermons*. The city characters in Restoration Comedy are habitually inarticulate in their amours. On such occasions they lapse into baby-talk.

For the rich merchants and men of business, the Restoration dramatists felt a brisk scorn. Jonson and Middleton had liked the City end of the town little enough; since when the citizens had aggravated their offences by enforcing, for eleven years, the tedious rectitudes of Cromwell's England. Even Pepys, who had many affiliations with them, despised such canting king-killers. He notes with disgust, one night in December, 1662, that the Duke's Theatre was "full of citizens, there hardly being a gentle man or woman in the house".[3] The hero of Etherege's *The Comical Revenge* is a Cavalier imprisoned by Cromwell and just released.[4] Aphra Behn's citizen-knight, recovering his intellectual balance at the end of *Sir Patient Fancy*, reverses everything in his past and becomes a Tory. "Methinks I find an Inclination," he says to Lady

Fancy, "to swear,—to curse myself and thee; nay, I'm so changed from what I was, that I think I could even approve of Monarchy and Church-discipline . . . and will turn Spark, they lead the merriest lives."[5] In Sir Patient's fall from Presbyterian grace the downfall of Cromwell's England is re-enacted.

Shadwell himself, although a Whig, ridicules the citizens in *Epsom Wells*. At that time Epsom was one of the spas at which persons of birth and fashion mingled with their crude imitators, the citizens and their wives. The pretentious civilities of Cheapside aping St James's are recorded in Shadwell's opening scene:

> BISK. I Vow it is a pleasurable Morning; the Waters tast so finely after being fudled last Night. Neighbour *Fribble*, here's a Pint to you.
> FRIBB. I'll pledge you Mr. *Bisket*, I have drunk eight already.
> MRS. BISK. How do the Waters agree with your Ladyship?
> MRS. WOOD. Oh Soveraignly; how many Cups are you arriv'd to?
> MRS. BISK. Truly six, and they pass so kindly—
> MRS. WOOD. 'Tis a delicious Morning.[6]

Shadwell repeatedly mocks the public endearments of the citizens and their wives, which were an offence against the manners of the time. Congreve also found the citizens' use of nicknames and expressions of affection fulsome and absurd. In one scene of Congreve's *Old Bachelor*, Fondlewife, dribbling amorousness, says goodbye to his wife Laetitia:

> FOND. That's my good Dear—Come kiss *Nykin* once more, and then get you in—So—Get you in, get you in. By, by.
> LAET. By *Nykin*.
> FOND. By Cocky.
> LAET. By *Nykin*.
> FOND. By Cocky, by, by.[7]

This duologue between Cocky and Nykin makes it clear why Millamant stipulates, as a condition of her marrying Mirabell, that he shall never "call her names". Restoration marriage followed a Spartan law. Just as he taught the youth of Sparta

to seize by stealth the food which was most nutritive to them;
so Lycurgus, in his Lacedemonian constitution, thinking secret
pleasures the most delightful, ordained that all matrimonial
endearments should be furtive. His hope was that married
people should not be satiated by each other, and would
accordingly come together with a greater force of desire for
each other's company.[8]

Alderman Gripe, in Wycherley's *Love in a Wood*, is an aged
City merchant as observed from the court end of the town:
a mean, sanctimonious rogue, but lecherous. He is bent on
gratifying his lechery at the lowest possible cost. Through
Mrs. Joyner he procures a wench called Lucy, but refuses to
spend any money on treats or feasts for her: "There can be no
entertainment to me more luscious and savoury than com-
munion with that little gentlewoman".[9] However, his fear of
scandal is greater than his generosity. In a very Wycherley-
like episode, in that it shows a deceiver pursuing a deception,
the women contrive to blackmail him out of five hundred
pounds without his enjoying Lucy at all. Alderman Smuggler,
in Farquhar's *Constant Couple*, is another instance of City
niggardliness and hypocrisy. He calls St. James's an "infectious
place" and an "unsanctified end of the town"; he professes
to find the very air of St. James's Park heathenish; yet he tries
to buy Lady Lurewell's favours with her own money, of which
he has cheated her. "I am an old fornicator", he explains,
"I'm not half so religious as I seem to be, you little rogue.
Why, I am disguised as I am; our sanctity is all outside, all
hypocrisy."[10] In the end he is trounced for his shifty behaviour
—the usual fate of aldermen in Restoration plays.

If in Restoration comedy the City represents the Roundhead
tradition, the countryside represents the Cavalier tradition,
in their view of which the dramatists were less positive. They
preferred the amenities of town-life; and Etherege, Shadwell
and Farquhar stress the boredom of the country. Gatty, the
heroine of Etherege's *She Would if She Could*, is happy to have
escaped to London, and has no patience with the few words
her sister Ariana speaks in defence of the country:

> Why, would it not make anyone mad to hear thee bewail the loss of the Country? Speak but one grave word more, and it shall be my daily Prayers thou may'st have a jealous Husband, and then you'll have enough of it I warrant you.[11]

The country, then, is a place to which jealous husbands exile their wives, so that they will have no opportunity for sexual adventures; or where, like Pinchwife in *The Country Wife*, they recruit wives who have not yet had that opportunity.

Describing how Lord Chesterfield expelled his wife from the court of Charles II to the country, where she remained surrounded by sad objects and impassable roads, the Count de Gramont speaks of the countryside as "little better than a gallows or a grave for young people".[12] "Ceremony, carried beyond all bearing," says Gramont, "is the grand characteristic of country people."[13] Thus Sir Wilfull Witwoud, always formal himself except when drunk or angry, is shocked by the informality of his brother's letters from London:

> I might expect this when you left off Honoured Brother; and hoping you are in good health, and so forth—To begin with a Rat me, Knight, I'm so sick of a last Night's Debauch.[14]

Harriet, the heroine of *The Man of Mode*, leaves for the country with tragic exclamations: "Emilia! Pity me, who am going to that sad place. Methinks I hear the hateful noise of Rooks already—Kaw, Kaw, Kaw—There's music in the worst Cry in London!"[15] Belinda's detestation of the country, in the same play, extends even to its flowers: "Do you think, my dear, I could be so loathsome to trick myself up with carnations and stock gillyflowers?" She never wears anything but exotic orange flowers and tuberoses.[16] Addressing a prospective husband, Wycherley's Hippolita accuses husbands of carrying off their wives, as soon as they have secured them, into Yorkshire, Wales, or Cornwall. Gerrard replies: "I see the air of this town, without the pleasures of it, is enough to infect women with an aversion for the country."[17] Admittedly, Hippolita, newly arrived from the village of Hackney, is

innocent enough in her prospect of London. She wants to see
Punch and Judy at Charing Cross, and eat cheese-cakes at the
Mulberry Garden; to try the cream buns at Islington and the
syllabubs at Vauxhall; to drink a pint of wine at a tavern and
hear "the organs and tongs" in Moorfields.[18]

The heroine of Shadwell's first play, *The Sullen Lovers*, speaks
of the country with a specific disdain: "to fill one's belly with
curds and cream, and stewed prunes, to eat honeycomb and
rashers of bacon at poor neighbour's houses, and rise by five
a clock in the morning to look to my diary".[19] Into the dialogue
in *Epsom Wells* between Lucia and Justice Clodpate ("an
immoderate hater of London") Shadwell inserts his customary
praises of London life and denigration of the country:

Luc. But if I could be content without being a Lady; I have vow'd
to spend all my life in *London*.

Clodp. Pox on her; live in *London* did she say? Death, have you
vow'd to live in *London* say you?

Luc. Yes, is that so wonderful? why people do really live no
where else; they breath, and move, and have a kind of insipid
dull being: but there is no life but in *London*.

Clodp. *London*! that sink of sin.

Luc. I believe there is no Village but sins as much in proportion
to the bigness; only your Country sins are something the
more block-headed sins.

Clodp. Madam, give me leave to ask you one question.

Luc. You may.

Clodp. Do you resolve to live honest?

Luc. 'Tis a familiar question; you had need to ask my leave first.

Clodp. Why? you may as reasonably expect to preserve your
health in a Pest-house, as your Chastity in that damn'd
lascivious Town.

Luc. You are rude, Sir.

Clodp. Come, Madam, plain dealing is a jewel. But can you
prefer an idle scandalous *London*-life, before a prety innocent
huswifely-life in the Country to look to your Family, and visit
your Neighbours?

Luc. To see my Ducks and Geese fed, and cram my own Chickens.
To have my Closet stink like a Pothecaries shop with Drugs
and Medicines, to administer to my sick Neighbours; and spoil
the next Quacks practice.[20]

The praise of London at the expense of the country in the opening scene of Shadwell's *Squire of Alsatia* is particularly apt, since it reflects the bumpkin Belfond Senior's infatuation with the unfamiliar city. He likes the London wine better than the dull March ale at home; well-dressed London women better than dairymaids and bare-foot strumpets; the streets full of coaches better than a yard full of dung-carts. "I could never have thought there had been such a gallant place as London", he says.[21] Shadwell's *Bury Fair* derides the small-town emulators of London fashions in Bury St. Edmunds, near Shadwell's native town, who are all enchanted by a French barber disguised as a count. Shadwell feels the greatest scorn for the provinces, the wits, fops and fine ladies there, and invents a string of human curiosities to justify his contempt. Although Bellamy, the hero of *Bury Fair*, is a lover of the country, in the course of a long debate on the respective merits of town and country his friend Wildish points out how misguided he is. Bellamy takes pleasure in reading the *Georgics* of Virgil, and contemplating the works of Nature. Wildish contemplates what he calls the chief works of Nature: "fine women; and the juice of the grape, well concocted by the sun".[22]

By the time Farquhar wrote *The Beaux' Stratagem* little new remained to be said on the subject of town and country, and it must be confessed that Farquhar said little new. Mrs. Sullen, a town-bred heiress, is married to a brutal squire who breakfasts on brandy, venison and strong beer. She complains to Dorinda, her sister-in-law, that her limbs were not made for leaping ditches or climbing over stiles; that she was never instructed in the "rural accomplishments" of drinking ale, playing at whist, and distilling rosemary water. In reply Dorinda asks why poets and philosophers have said that the country is the place where happiness is to be found. To this Mrs. Sullen answers:

> Because they wanted Money, Child, to find out the Pleasures of the Town. Did you ever see a Poet or Philosopher worth Ten thousand Pound? If you can show me such a Man, I'll lay you Fifty Pound you'll find him somewhere within the weekly Bills.[23]

It will be noted that Etherege, Shadwell and Farquhar take the Epicurean view that the urban stage of civilisation is an advance. Epicurus had a garden, but a garden not far outside Athens.

From the point of view of the mode the country stood for an ale-drinking, whist-playing tedium; yet from the point of view of honour it stood for a great deal more. The country was where the traditional decencies of Stuart England persisted. Etherege, Shadwell and Farquhar concede as much in making their pure heroines country-bred girls. Of all the comic dramatists of the time Congreve, who conveys a delicate perception of natural scenery in his poems and translations, has most to say in favour of the rural virtues. Miss Prue, in *Love for Love*, comes to London in a flutter of lavender and maidenly daydreams, only to be corrupted by the hard, insincere London people. She is taught to call her stepmother "Madam" and not to use the coarse word "Smocks". Mr. Tattle, who hopes to seduce Prue, protests: "Oh Madam; you are too severe upon Miss; you must not find fault with her pretty simplicity, it becomes her strangely—pretty Miss, don't let them persuade you out of your innocency." Her stepmother, Mrs. Foresight, replies, "Oh, demn you, you Toad—I wish you don't persuade her out of her Innocency."[24] Mrs. Foresight, trusting that he will eventually marry Prue, then leaves Tattle alone with her. At once he instructs her in the ways of London life:

> Your Words must contradict your Thoughts; but your Actions may contradict your Words. So, when I ask you, if you can love me, you must say no, but you must love me too—If I tell you you are handsome, you must deny it, and say I flatter you—But you must think your self more charming than I speak you:—And like me, for the Beauty which I say you have, as much as if I had it my self—If I ask you to kiss me, you must be angry, but you must not refuse me. If I ask you for more, you must be more angry,—but more complying; and as soon as ever I make you say you'll cry out, you must be sure to hold your Tongue.[25]

Prue is so infatuated with the sham splendours of Tattle

that she has no time at all for the worthy tar, Ben Legend, when he comes to woo her:

> MISS. But I'm sure it is not so, for I'll speak sooner than you should believe that; and I'll speak Truth, tho' one should always tell a Lie to a Man; and I don't care, let my Father do what he will; I'm too big to be whipt, so I'll tell you plainly, I don't like you, nor love you at all, nor ever will, that's more: So, there's your Answer for you; and don't trouble me no more, you ugly thing.[26]

The final stage in Prue's lesson comes when Tattle teaches her, as directly as possible, the superficiality of town amours:

> TATT. O fie; what, we must not love one another now—Pshaw, that would be a foolish thing indeed—Fie, fie, you're a Woman now, and must think of a new Man every Morning, and forget him every Night—No, no, to marry is to be a Child again, and play with the same Rattle always: O fie, marrying is a paw thing.
>
> MISS. Well, but don't you love me as well as you did last Night then?[27]

At the end of the play Prue, forsaking her country-bred pieties, is discovered stamping her small feet and defying her father like a second Mrs. Foresight: "For now my mind is set upon a Man, I will have a Man some way or other."[28] Meanwhile the fashionable people, as so often happens in Restoration Comedy, fall victims to their own duplicity. By a mistake which, as Dr. Johnson remarks, is not very probably contrived, Mr. Tattle and Mrs. Frail marry each other whilst both are disguised as other persons:

> MRS. FRAIL. O, Sister, the most unlucky Accident.
> MRS. FORE. What's the Matter?
> TATT. O, the two most unfortunate poor Creatures in the World we are.
> FORE. Bless us! How so?
> MRS. FRAIL. Ah Mr. *Tattle* and I, poor Mr. *Tattle* and I are—I can't speak it out.
> TATT. Nor I—poor Mrs. Frail and I are—

MRS. FRAIL. . . . Married.

MRS. FORE. Married! How?

TATT. Suddenly—before we knew where we were—that Villain *Jeremy*, by the help of Disguises, trickt us into one another.[29]

Thus Prue is recruited to a world of profitless artifice and dissimulation. In *The Way of the World*, Sir Wilfull Witwoud, morally a much more admirable character than Mirabell, retains his bumpkin honesty to the last. Magnanimously he makes Millamant over to Mirabell—magnanimously and with relief, since he is terrified by her sophistication:

> 'Sheart, Aunt, I have no mind to marry. My cousin's a fine Lady, and the Gentleman loves her, and she loves him, and they deserve one another; my resolution is to see Foreign Parts—I have set on it—and when I'm set on't, I must do't.[30]

In its lowest manifestations, such as the conduct of Mr. Tattle, the supposed good breeding of London people becomes a system of affected observances. One part of the system is a showy civility, manifestly insincere, and practised out of mere loquacity, as by Mr. Brisk in Congreve's *The Double Dealer*:

> Oh, my dear Mellefont, let me perish, if thou art not the Soul of Conversation, the very Essence of Wit, and Spirit of Wine. The Deuce take me if there were three good things said, or understood, since thy Amputation from the Body of our Society.[31]

Another part of the system is a petty over-attention to the attitudes of the body and their expressiveness. In such manuals of deportment as Lauze's *Apologie de la Danse*, gentlemen were taught how to make the bow in passing—the hat removed with the right hand and transferred to the left, where it was held against the hip in a careless manner, the inside turned inwards—and the more respectful bow, in which the right arm was extended forward and downward towards the ground, the palm of the hand uppermost, but not carried beyond the line of the body.

The literature of deportment for women was yet larger, and may be summed up in the words of Medley in *The Man of Mode*:

> Then there is the Art of affectation, written by a late beauty of Quality, teaching you to draw up your Breasts, stretch up your neck, to thrust out your Breech, to play with your Head, to toss up your Nose, to bite your Lips, to turn up your Eyes, to speak in a silly soft tone of a Voice, and use all the Foolish French Words that will infallibly make your person and conversation charming.[32]

Heartfree is by no means charmed by such behaviour on the part of Lady Fancyfull in *The Provoked Wife*, whom he accuses of having become, in spite of her natural loveliness, the pity of men and the jest of women:

> There is not a Feature in your Face, but you have found a way to teach it some affected Convulsion; your Feet, your Hands, your very Finger Ends are directed never to move without some ridiculous Air or other; and your Language is a suitable Trumpet, to draw people's Eyes upon the Raree-show.[33]

Shadwell's tomboy heroine, Gertrude Oldwit, has no patience with such antics:

> I know no breeding necessary, but Discretion to distinguish Company and occasions; and Common Sence, to entertain persons according to their Ranks; besides making a Courtesie not awkwardly, and walking with one's Toes out.[34]

She thinks that a woman can look after the affairs of her family and her household, and discharge all the offices of a good wife, without learning French: "and this is all I desire to arrive at". In her opinion, a woman of mode, with her elaborate compliments and artificial conversation and French, is "good for no more than a dancing mare, to be led about and shown". Compliments she considers to be "a flam, a mere flam". She spurns the insincerities of the beau monde, embracing instead the ponderous but honest courtesies of the countryside.

Such speeches as Gertrude's show that England was not utterly mannered and worldly during these years. It is pleasant to find that in 1674, the year of the composition of Wycherley's misanthropic *Country Wife*, a saintly gentleman was bequeathing his best hat in Teddington; the housekeeper and the laundry-maid witnessing the will of Sir Orlando Bridgeman's chaplain, Thomas Traherne. Traherne divided up his personal fortune into units of five shillings and half a crown, to leave something to as many people as possible. He left his books and his best hat to his brother Philip. The disposal of his old hat he left to his executors. For his patroness Susanna Hopton he had already written his *Centuries of Meditation*. At Kington, near Credenhill, Susanna Hopton had surrounded herself with a religious community of which Traherne had become spiritual director. Her husband, the busy Chief Justice of Charles II, stood outside her religious life. Five times a day she said her prayers, and she kept all fasts. She went over her accounts daily, so that she might give superabundance to the poor. Susanna Hopton gives one an insight into the life led by such Restoration country-folk as Harriet's mother in *The Man of Mode*; sitting by the fat carved swags of their treacle-coloured chimney-pieces, in their dark-panelled, galleried halls. The grave and sober shunned London. Sir William Temple lived for five years in Sheen without once going to London, although he was almost within sight of it, and had a house there always ready to receive him.[35]

Country people are figures of fun in Restoration Comedy because of their inelegance and their whimsical old-fashioned ways; yet they are curiously respected too, for their conservative observance of the old Cavalier rectitudes. The scruples and decorums of the early seventeenth century—the concepts of Honour which are found in the verse of Lovelace and Cowley— persisted in the heroic tragedy of the Restoration, and indeed underlie much of the comedy. The components of Honour were steadfastness, honesty and a punctilious self-respect. As Lady Vaine says in Shadwell's *Sullen Lovers*: "a Lady without virtue and honour is altogether as detestable as a gentleman without wit or courage".[36] Loveless's conduct in *The Relapse*, when he wounds Lord Foppington for having

insulted Amanda, reminds us that men at that time wore not
only ruffles and frills but swords as well, and sometimes used
them. The sense of chivalry and family honour is as important
in the romantic section of Etherege's first comedy, *The Comical
Revenge*, as it is in the plays of Ford or Fletcher. Colonel
Bruce, a Cavalier imprisoned by Cromwell and just released,
is almost a personification of chivalry. He finds that his mistress,
Graciana, has been unfaithful to him, but such is his esteem for
her family that at the end of the play he marries her sister
instead.

Beaufort, who has won Graciana from Bruce, insists on
fighting a duel with him: he thinks the situation calls for a
duel. Lovis regards his sister's jilting of Bruce as a family
fault for which he tries to atone. A chain of chivalrous para-
doxes follows. For honourable reasons Bruce, an expert swords-
man, refuses to fight Beaufort. For equally honourable reasons
Beaufort, determined to give Bruce his chance of revenge,
taunts Bruce into fighting:

> Think on thy neglected Love:
> Think on the beauteous *Graciana's* eyes;
> 'Tis I have robbed you of that glorious prize.

Bruce fights, but allows Beaufort to disarm him. Beaufort
returns Bruce's sword. To demonstrate his courage, Bruce
falls upon it. With a generous hyperbole Beaufort exclaims,
"Hold gallant man! Honour itself does bleed!" He rounds
on Graciana:

> Was there no way his constancy to prove
> But by your own inconstancy in Love?[37]

Fortunately for the game little Aurelia (who, although secretly
in love with Bruce, had to act as the messenger of his love for
Graciana) Bruce survives, and is tended by her, which gives
rise to some absurd and pretty scenes. The comedy concludes,
like a comedy of the preceding age, with the joint marriages
of Aurelia to Bruce and Graciana to Beaufort.

Aphra Behn sees the honour of the family as the chief
safeguard of the women in it. When, in her *Town Fop*, Lord
Plotwell disunites his family, he destroys the system of mutual
support on which the security of the women depends. As a
consequence, his sweet, pert young niece Phyllis is ruined by Sir
Timothy Tawdrey, who says, "We have found it incommode
and loss of time to make long addresses," and forthwith
debauches her.

Wycherley has less respect for the conventions of family
honour than Etherege or Aphra Behn. One looks in vain for
a Brutus or a Virginius in the plays of Wycherley. Although
there is some return to the heroic sentiment of Jacobean tragedy
in *The Gentleman Dancing Master*, in which Hippolita has
reason to fear that her father, because of his "strictness and
punctilios", may kill her as "the shame and stain of his honour
and family", this heroic sentiment (which, indeed, persisted
in Restoration tragedy) is dismissed as ridiculous and suitable
only to Hippolita's father, who is an absurd aper of Spanish
manners.

There is an everlasting babble of honour in Wycherley's
Country Wife; mainly on the lips of the wholly dishonourable
Lady Fidget and the other furtive Bacchae of the play. Pinchwife, the foolish, passionate man, comes sword-in-hand to
force Horner to marry his sister, whom he mistakenly believes
Horner to have seduced. Horner has seduced, in fact, not
Pinchwife's sister but his wife; which lends irony to Pinchwife's
words when he says: "a woman's injured honour, no more than
a man's, can be satisfied or repaired by any but him that first
wronged it".[38] By his own standards, Horner does repair
Mrs. Pinchwife's honour by preserving her from discovery; for
he thinks that "honour, like beauty now, only depends on
the opinion of others".[39] Wycherley himself remarks, in the
book of *Maxims* he wrote in his old age—bitter distillations of
his long experience—that reputation is oftener founded on "the
manner and art we use to appear honest" than on "any true
or solid merit".[40] Like *The Country Wife*, Wycherley's *Plain
Dealer* is mainly concerned with the frauds and knaveries

of those who appear to be honourable, but really think, with
Lucy in *The Country Wife*:

> But what a Divil is this honour! 'tis sure a disease in the head,
> like the Megrim, or Falling-sickness, that always hurries People
> away to do themselves mischief; Men lose their lives by it:
> Women, what's dearer to 'em, their love, the life of life.[41]

With the traditions of Caroline honour, calling for self-
restraint and even self-sacrifice, the mode of Restoration times,
which at least in its early stages incorporated a cult of self-
indulgence, had little to do. Yet the voice of the former Cavaliers was immersed in the general music of the Restoration;
and Caroline honour, like one singer's notes sustained and
discernible in the concord of the choir, still startled the ear.
Shadwell, who makes no claim to be a man of mode, has little
enthusiasm for fashionable debauchery. Sarcastically he makes
one of his rakes in *Epsom Wells* say to another, "Oh let me kiss
that hand: he must be an illustrious man whose hand shakes
at twenty-two".[42] In accordance with Shadwell's own tastes,
his heroine Carolina, in *Epsom Wells*, is an old-fashioned girl.
A brisk and disrespectful style of courtship had developed
during the early years of the Restoration. As Dorset wrote:

> We live in an Age that's more civil and wise
> Than to follow the Rules of Romances.[43]

Carolina has no patience with this new libertine fashion of
wooing. She would prefer even the silliest artificialities of the
old, formal courtship: "Scribbling your passion in glass
windows, and wearing my colours continually, I can better
endure."[44]

In Aphra Behn's *The Town Fop*, debauchery is represented
as being the way of life of Sir Timothy Tawdrey; not of her
hero Bellmour, with whom it is only an aberration. Unlike
most of Aphra Behn's fops, who are likable clowns, Sir Timothy
is vicious. At the beginning of the play he makes an attempt
on Bellmour's secret mistress, Celinda, although regretting

that she "is quite spoiled for want of town education". His own town education consists of gambling and whoring. With ridiculous assurance he informs Bellmour that he intends to marry Celinda. Bellmour exclaims, "How, sir, you marry fair Celinda!" Mistaking Bellmour's surprise, Sir Timothy answers: "Ay, Frank, ay. Is she not a pretty little plump white rogue, ha?" Bellmour's jealousy breaks through his modish surface: "And canst thou think this beauty meant for thee, dull common man?"

Sir Timothy does not challenge Bellmour. Instead he urges Sham, one of his henchmen, to fight him. "Sham," he says, "thou art a poor dog, and 'tis no matter if the world were well rid of thee."[45]

Sir Timothy's promiscuity among prostitutes other than herself has already alarmed his mistress, Mrs. Flauntit, with the fear that he will infect her with the pox: "I'm in no small danger of getting the foul disease by your lewdness."[46] This is the man who, because of the disintegration of Bellmour's family, is able to marry Bellmour's sister Phyllis. Sir Timothy intends to continue to frequent Mrs. Flauntit after the marriage. "Go home and expect me", he says. "Thou'lt have me all to thyself within this day or two."[47] It is a grim ending to a play, and Aphra Behn's shrewish feminist comment on a world run by men.

In Wycherley's contempt for the vapid young men of *Love in a Wood*, whose misdeeds he recounts without liking, there is a burly sarcastic strength. No more than Shadwell or Aphra Behn does he relish young sparks who spend their days "drinking to engender wit" and their nights hunting women in St. James's Park. The exacting standard of their drinking is suggested by Wycherley's Mr. Ranger, when he reassuringly says, "We have drunk yet but our bottle apiece," adding that Mr. Vincent "dares not look a woman in the face under three bottles".[48] When Mr. Vincent has had his three bottles, Wycherley's little group of wits rambles out into the park. Mr. Ranger thinks there are advantages in the night-courtship they practise there: "A man may bring his bashful wench, and not have her put out of countenance by the impudent honest women of the town."[49] In the park Mr. Ranger meets his own mistress by mistake and attempts to ravish her, not troubling to take her mask off first:

> RANGER. Since you will not speak, I'll try if you will squeak. (*Goes to throw her down, she squeaks.*)

Such are the graceful encounters in St. James's Park.[50]

The distinction between mode and honour is important in the discussions, frequent in Restoration Comedy, concerning the education of gentlemen. Bruce and Longvil, in the opening scene of Shadwell's *Virtuoso*, favour a greater strictness in the early training of a man of fashion. They lament that "'tis accounted pedantry for a gentleman to spell", and agree in deploring two classes of young men: the fops and the debauchees. The fops are "first instructed by ignorant, young, household pedants, who dare not whip the dunces, their pupils, for fear of their lady mothers", and then "before they can construe and parse they are sent into France". The debauchees "early break loose from discipline and at sixteen, forsooth, set up for men of the town":

> BRUCE. Such as come Drunk and Screaming into a Playhouse and stand upon the Benches and toss their full Periwigs and empty Heads and with their shrill unbroken Pipes cry, "*Damn me, this is a Damned Play. Prethee, let's to a Whore, Jack*". . . .
> LONGVIL. Heaven be praised, these Youths, like untimely Fruit, are like to be rotten before they are ripe.

In *The Squire of Alsatia*, a dramatic debate on two systems of education, Shadwell adopts laxer principles than in *The Virtuoso*. Belfond Senior, bred by his father with "great rigour and severity", becomes "lewd, abominably vicious and obstinate". Belfond Junior, bred by his uncle with "tenderness and liberty", becomes "of excellent disposition and temper". Belfond Senior, slipping away from his harsh father, plunges into Alsatia (an area between the Temple and Salisbury Square at that time conferring immunity from arrest upon its inhabitants, and therefore thick with debtors, rogues and thieves) and starts to squander the estate entailed upon him. He is reclaimed by Belfond Junior, who has always been allowed more freedom, and consequently uses it with good sense. The facile argument for indulgence snatches at educational theories which were in the air at the time and were pinned down by John Locke in his *Thoughts concerning Education* four years later.

When Belfond Senior is forcibly shown how he has been deceived by his spurious friends and even more spurious mistress in Alsatia, he wakes up like Bottom in *A Midsummer Night's Dream*: "What, are all these rogues? And that a whore? and am I cheated?"[51] Shocked by the results of the training he has given Belfond Senior, his father decides to loosen his control in future. He resolves to have a good time himself too—to throw off with the restraints he has put on his son the restraints which he has put on himself: "I'll come up to London, feast and revel, and never take a minute's care while I breathe again."[52] Some people may be less pleased with Belfond Junior than Shadwell obviously is himself. It seems that the younger brother's freedom has not taught him to be frank and honourable, but only to wheedle others when it suits his purpose, and to behave with a hard selfishness when there is nothing to be gained. To his uncle and his father he is abjectly ingratiating, but when it comes to discarding a mistress he behaves without a trace of decent sentiment:

> Why, you were not married to me: I took no lease of your frail tenement: I was but a tenant at my own will.[53]

Most often in Restoration Comedy, Honour is regarded as a traditional and native quality; Mode as something new-fangled and Frenchified. Honour has all the conservatism of the Just Cause in Aristophanes's *Clouds*. Bruce and Longvil, like Aristophanes's Just Cause, cry up the ancient system of education, when the boys from the same quarter of the town marched in good order through the streets to the school of the harp-master, lightly clad and in a body, though the snow fell thick as flour; ran races with modest rivals beneath the sacred olives, crowned with white reeds; had clear complexions, broad shoulders and little lewdness. In the same terms Wycherley objects to Mr. Paris, the brewer's foppish son in *The Gentleman Dancing Master*, who has returned from Paris infected alike with the pox and with French manners—"So perfect a Frenchman", says the hero of the play, "that the draymen of your father's own brewhouse would be ready to knock thee on the head."[54]

The French settlers at the court of Charles II are censured in his memoirs by one of their number, the Count de Gramont. He says that they strove to outdo each other in folly and extravagance and treated the English as foreigners in their own country. Yet many of the English nobility were willing to comply with them. St. Évremond lived in London for more than forty years without needing, or troubling, to write his letters in English. With Buckingham and Ormonde, St. Albans and Arlington, he corresponded in his native language. The English Mounsieurs and the *Précieuses* of Restoration Comedy suggest that there was some measure of fairly brainless copying of French modes amongst the fashionable people of the time. Dryden's Melantha drains French plays and romances for new words for her daily conversation. Every morning her maid brings her a list of French phrases to use on her visits. Without the list, Melantha says, her language would be "threadbare *et usé*, and fit for nothing but to be thrown to peasants".[55] Vanbrugh's Lady Fancyful forms her deportment on the model of her Parisian *fille de chambre*. Hearing that French ladies recruit their lovers by the hundred, Lady Fancyful observes: "Well, strike me dead, I think they have *le goût bon*."[56]

Shadwell's Lady Fantast, although she has never been in France, has "often bewailed the not having the honour to be born French".[57] Her daughter, Mrs. Fantast, so tricks out her conversation with bad French that her father remarks: "Have a care of losing your English before you have gotten another language." Mrs. Fantast, who thinks that the English gentry look like tradesmen compared with the French *noblesse*, contracts to marry a French barber pretending to be a count: Wycherley's Mr. Paris goes further than Mrs. Fantast, in that he has started to speak his native English with a French sentence-structure. He delights in speaking English "agreeably ill", and refers to his fellow-countrymen as "You English". He is not like Gerrard, the hero of the play, who has "been abroad as much as any man, and does not make the least show of it"—no more show than Wycherley himself, who was educated in France. The comic dramatists of the Restoration, who had little admiration for the French and still less for the English imitators of the French, deplored such slavishness.

Thus in Etherege's *Man of Mode* the substantial, although malevolently deployed, accomplishments of Dorimant are contrasted with the French froth of his imitator, Sir Fopling Flutter. Sir Fopling travels in the style of a Grand Seigneur, with a retinue of six footmen and a page. He would rather have the conversation of a French lackey than of an English Esquire. He refuses to feel jealousy because "it is not French, it is not French at all". No Englishman, he says, advising Dorimant to employ a French valet, knows how to tie a ribbon. Like Congreve's Valentine, who reads Seneca and Epictetus in his chamber, Dorimant is a thoroughly literate hero. Sir Fopling apes Dorimant's performance but cannot perceive that the performance is only the excrescence of Dorimant's will and intellect. Although a good-humoured fellow, Sir Fopling is quite empty-headed; in this he differs from the far from unintelligent Lord Foppington, to whom he had the glory of giving rise. "Writing, madam", says Sir Fopling, "is a mechanical part of wit. A gentleman should never go beyond a song or a billet." Excusing his clumsy dancing, he explains: "I have sat up so damned late, and drunk so cursed hard, since I came to this lewd town, that I am fit for nothing. . . . Pox on this debauchery!" He vastly admires Dorimant, and takes the fiddles round to waken him at four in the morning (so causing considerable embarrassment to Belinda). He would much rather talk to Dorimant than to the ladies, of whom, in spite of his avowals, he is shy. He says that he is reserving himself: "An intrigue now would be but a temptation to me to throw away that vigour on one, which I mean shall shortly make my court to the whole sex in a ballet." He is as self-enamoured as Dorimant, but less confidently. Sententiously he complains of the lack of a looking glass in Dorimant's sitting room: "In a glass a man may entertain himself and correct the errors of his motion and his dress." Dorimant needs no looking glass in order to be Dorimant. That is why Harriet can make something more of him than a man of mode.

Like his presumed original, the Earl of Rochester, Dorimant has an intellectual vigour equally adaptable to good and ill. Rochester's concern was with an inner resolution; Dorimant's concern is to find some outward purpose which will not pall upon him. At the end of *The Man of Mode* Harriet has some hopes of taming Dorimant the Hobbesian wolf-man, and bringing him within the bounds of the social decencies. As in Botticelli's painting, wise Pallas grasps the centaur by the hair. Like the Unicorn of medieval legend, symbol of energy and generation, Dorimant must subside in the lap of a virgin before he can be reclaimed from the ferocity of his ways.

Congreve's *Way of the World* carries to a conclusion this theme, left open at the end of *The Man of Mode*, of the reclaimed rake. All the unicorns come trooping in to Millamant, only too anxious to lay down their arms in her maiden lap, but she tells them to go away. She is waiting for a completely white Unicorn. She is the rosebush of *The Romance of the Rose*: everybody wants her roses and she would not know what to do were it not for the extremely deliberate and directed display of apparent capriciousness and arrogance towards men by which Millamant is able to keep them at the distance needed for the moral protection of so enticing a young being; yet without seeming prudish or narrow for doing so. She loves to be cruel, she tells Mirabell, but she is cruel only to him, and only as a punishment for his shifty actions. As Mirabell himself tells her, she affects a cruelty which is not in her nature.

Although Mirabell presents himself to Millamant as a person of sturdy sincerity, he is, in fact, the least sincere and the most devious of men; and Millamant knows this well. The sidelong amours he pursues with such ladies as her old aunt and Mrs. Fainall do not please Millamant, nor do his other slynesses; so that before she will admit him to her rose-garden—to disturb the good order of that tranquil milieu with the wolf-pack of his wishes—she exacts some whimsically malicious penalties. The moral aspect of the play is to be seen in the way that the modish but dissolute Mirabell is presented not as admirable in himself as he stands, but as hitherto wasted intelligence ready for reclamation. Millamant herself tends, a vestal virgin, the patrician flame of Caroline honour. Her respect for the traditional decencies is shown in her surprise at Mirabell's finding it necessary, in his provisoes, to tell her not to go to the play in a mask, not to drink spirits and not to toast men:

> O horrid Proviso's! Filthy strong waters! I toast Fellows—odious men! I hate your odious Proviso's.[58]

In Cibber's *Love's Last Shift* the Unicorn, who has been to the woods again, is lured back to the sanctity of the virtuous lap. The prodigal husband, Loveless, returns to the safe arms of his wife Amanda. After five months of marriage he had left her. "The World to me", he says, "is a garden stock'd with all sorts of Fruit, where the greatest Pleasure we can take is in the Variety of Taste. But a wife is an eternal Apple-tree."[59] The separation has lasted ten years, Loveless has spent the time in costly riot, mortgaging his estate, making the tour of Europe, and finally returning to England so poor and shameless that he solicits one of his old friends for a guinea to buy a dinner. During all those years Amanda, dressed all the time in mourning, has been faithful to her memories of Loveless. As if this sweet improbability did not in itself strain the audience's credulity enough, Cibber makes the husband for whom she has been breaking her heart for ten years one of the most oafish characters in Restoration Comedy. He says that it was the staleness of Amanda's love that drove him abroad. Hearing the rumour of her having died of grief at his wild behaviour, he observes: "Why, faith, she was a good-natured fool, that's the truth on't. Well! rest her soul!" Loveless is Etherege's Dorimant or Aphra Behn's Wilding, sodden and coarsened: a fatal brute rather than a fatal man, his mind emerging from his swinish immersions from time to time only long enough to snatch at passing gratifications.

Amanda, although innocent, is no fool. She has an amused recognition of the many contradictions inherent in being a woman. "'Tis observed", she says, "that a bragging Lover and an over-shy Lady are the farthest from what they would seem; the one is as seldom known to receive a Favour, as the other to resist an Opportunity".[60] Thus the pretty moralist is able to overcome her scruples over Young Worthy's plan for her conquest of Loveless. Loveless is to be brought to her at night, she passing upon him as an unknown mistress who has mistaken his identity; so that he shall cuckold himself and clandestinely enjoy his own wife. This is love's last shift, to teach Loveless that his objection to Virtue is merely an irrational prejudice. Having made up her mind to follow Young Worthy's plan, Amanda asks Hillaria if she should follow it:

> For though I'm his wife, yet while he loves me not as such, I encourage an unlawful Passion; and though the Act be safe, yet his Intent is criminal. How can I answer this?

Hillaria, a little impatient with the almost theological subtleties of Amanda's conscience, in the end replies: "If you succeed, I suppose you will easily forgive your guilt in the undertaking."[61] In his old age Cibber was a close friend of Samuel Richardson. Perhaps the quaint moral perplexities of Amanda anticipate those of Pamela and Clarissa.

The honest fraud succeeds. It must have done Loveless a great deal of good, because the morning after the pious deception he enters spruce, urbane and talking philosophy. Amanda, still disguised, asks him if he never felt the constraints

of conscience, nor remorse for his broken vows.[62] Standing
in a fixed posture, Loveless replies:

> That you should ask me this, confounds my Reason. And yet
> your Words are utter'd with such a powerful Accent, they have
> awakened my Soul, and strike my Thoughts with Horror and
> Remorse . . . Oh! thou hast rouz'd me from my deep Lethargy of
> Vice!

As we shall see, Sir John Vanbrugh found Loveless's conversion
too pat and too abrupt to be convincing, especially since
Loveless gains so much by it. Amanda raises Loveless from
squalor, reclothes him, and redeems the mortgage on his estate.
The fatted calf dies for love of him.

Vanbrugh makes the transition from mode to honour a
more considered one. Between *Love's Last Shift* and Vanbrugh's
sequel, *The Relapse*, we are to imagine an interval which Loveless has spent decently in the country with Amanda, a Theseus
both safeguarded and constrained by Ariadne's loving thread.
The main plot of *The Relapse* is founded upon Loveless's
remark in *Love's Last Shift*: "Who can boast a victory, when they
have no foe to conquer?" Confident in his faithfulness, Loveless decides to venture the risks of the town.

> But since, against my Will, I'm dragg'd once more to that
> uneasie Theatre of Noise, I am resolv'd to make such use on't, as
> shall convince you 'tis an old cast Mistress, who has been so lavish
> of her Favours, she's now grown Bankrupt of her Charms, and
> has not one Allurement left to move me.[63]

Almost at once he relapses, with Amanda's cousin, the young
widow Berinthia. Amanda is right in supposing him too bold
in quitting the country, the "little soft retreat" where, he
says:

> My life glides on, and all is well within.[64]

At the same time Amanda's own virtue is put to the test,
in an extreme way. She is at once confronted with the most

positive evidence of her husband's adultery—evidence supplied
by the treacherous Berinthia herself—and warmly besieged
by Mr. Worthy, for whom Berinthia tries to procure her.
For one uneasy and fatal moment all is nearly lost:

> AMANDA. O whither am I going? Help, Heaven, or I am lost.
> WORTHY. Stand Neuter, gods, this once I do invoke you.
> AMANDA. Then save me, Vertue, and the Glory's thine.
> WORTHY. Nay, never strive.
> AMANDA. I will; and Conquer too. My Forces rally bravely to my
> aid (*breaking from him*), and thus I gain the Day.[65]

Amanda is no sexual suffragette. She does not think that
because her husband is an adulterer she should herself solicit
a like ugly name. She is not so much her husband's creature
that her virtue depends on his actions. Her honour is not a
relative thing, but absolute to her self-respect. She will not in
mere spitefulness derange her own emotional integrity. Even
Mr. Worthy esteems her the more for her firmness of principle:
"Sure there's divinity about her; and she's dispensed some
portion on't to me." To this divinity the Unicorn Loveless is
lured back at the end of the play. "I am too fond of my own
wife", he tells Lord Foppington, "to have the least inclination for yours."

Farquhar's Sir Harry Wildair is a further example of a
modish rake reclaimed by a woman who embodies the traditions of Caroline honour. Like Loveless, Sir Harry abandons
his chaste and constant wife for the sake of variety, and is only
brought back to her by the stratagem of her mock-death.
The stratagem leads her to appear in *Sir Harry Wildair* disguised
as her own ghost. Sir Harry, convinced that his wife is dead,
confronts the ghost with his habitual nonchalance:

> Blood, I'll speak to 't. Vous, Mlle. Ghost, parle-vous *François*?
> No? Hark ye, Mrs. Ghost, will your Ladyship be pleas'd to
> inform us who you are, that we may pay you the Respect due
> to your Quality?
> GHOST. I am the Spirit of your departed Wife.

SIR HARRY. Are you faith? Why then here's the Body of thy living Husband, and stand me if you dare. (*Runs to her and Embraces her.*) Ha! 'tis Substance I'm sure. But hold, Lady Ghost, stand off a little, and tell me in good earnest now, Whether you are alive or dead?

ANGELICA (*Throwing off her Shroud*). Alive! Alive! (*throws her Arms about his Neck*) and never live so much as in this moment.[66]

Farquhar gives a great deal of thought to the subject of honourable marriage in *Sir Harry Wildair*, contrasting with it the adulteries of Lady Lurewell. In the Fourth Act, Sir Harry teases the jealous Lady Lurewell by describing the decorous bliss of his marriage; yet, like Loveless, he abandons his paragon for a fashionable promiscuity, and is only brought back to her by his seeming forfeiture of her.

Ariadne at once rescues and tethers Theseus, defining his course. The heroines of Restoration Comedy, who are almost always virtuous women in the strictest and most traditional sense, hold the heroes to the terms of Caroline honour. In vain does Sir Harry Wildair profess to scorn Honour as "a very troublesome and impertinent thing", so denying most of the assumptions on which Restoration Comedy is based:

Look ye, my lord, when you and I were under the Tuition of our Governors, and convers'd only with old *Cicero, Livy, Virgil, Plutarch* and the like; why then such a Man was a Villain, and such a one was a Man of Honour. But now, that I have known the Court, a little of what they call the *Beau-monde*, and the *Belle esprit*, I find that Honour looks as ridiculous as *Roman* buskins on your Lordship, or my full Peruke upon *Scipio Africanus*.[67]

In vain he brags, since his wife Angelica softly draws him back to the old decencies, as Millamant draws back Mirabell. Blunt Thomas Shadwell had established the pattern at the beginning of the era—crudely observing, one supposes, the life around him. His heroines invariably reject the man of mode in favour of the man of honour.

Having made the hero of *The Feigned Courtesans*—the faithful Sir Harry Fillamour—a Man of Honour, Aphra Behn reverted to the Man of Mode in *The City Heiress*.[68] Yet *The City Heiress* is a more powerful persuasive to the life of Honour than *The*

Feigned Courtesans, since in it the disasters brought about by the Mode are allowed to speak for themselves. To the sombre ending of *The City Heiress*, as to many of Mrs. Behn's final scenes, the last words of Thackeray's *Vanity Fair* could well be applied: "Which of us is happy in this world? Which of us has his desire, or, having it, is satisfied?" The hero, Tom Wilding (based on Etherege's Dorimant, and perhaps also a little on Aphra Behn's lover, John Hoyle), is ruthless, perverse, and seemingly irresistible to women. He glories in the illicit:

> The stealths of Love, the midnight kind Admittance,
> The gloomy Bed, the soft breath'd murmuring Passion;
> Ah, who can guess at Joys thus snatch'd by parcels?
> The difficulty makes us always wishing,
> Whilst on thy part, fear makes still some resistance;
> And every Blessing seems a kind of Rape.[69]

Hearing these words, Sir Anthony Merriwill, the old rake of the play, mutters: "A Divine Fellow that; just of my religion." Wilding speaks of "the busy afflictions of the day and the debauches of the tedious night". He dislikes the notion of marriage: "How pleasant to drink when a man's dry! The rest is but dully sipping on." But he has promised his mistress that he will marry a rich wife in order to pay his mistress an allowance.

Wilding's uncle Sir Timothy Treat-All, a satirical portrait of the Whig leader Shaftesbury, is thinking of marrying a widow called Lady Galliard. Wilding finds this foolish, and also damaging to Wilding's own interests. He assumes that Lady Galliard wishes to marry Sir Timothy only to provide cover for the effects of her own amours, and mockingly advises her not to do so. His uncle, he says, is "a fellow who will not so much as serve you for a cloak, he is so visibly and undeniably impotent".[70] Wilding swiftly goes on to seduce Lady Galliard himself:

> L. GAL. Oh, why were all the Charms of speaking given to that false Tongue that makes no better use of 'em?—I'll hear no more of your inchanting Reasons.

WILD. You must.
L. GAL. I will not.
WILD. Indeed you must.
L. GAL. By all the Powers above—
WILD. By all the Powers of Love you'll break your Oath, unless
you swear this Night to let me see you.
L. GAL. This night.
WILD. This very night.
L. GAL. I'd die first—At what Hour?

Another but less welcome attempt on Lady Galliard is
made by Sir Charles Merriwill who is never bold with ladies
unless drunk, and when drunk outrageous. Sir Charles is
encouraged in his enormities of bad manners by his uncle,
Sir Anthony Merriwill, who is always zealous in mischief.
Briskly Sir Charles woos Lady Galliard:

L. GALL. I'll call for help.
SIR. C. You need not, you'll do my business better alone.[71]

Wilding, always malevolent towards his fair prey, loses patience
with Lady Galliard and Sir Charles, and marries Charlotte,
the city heiress, mainly to spite Lady Galliard. Lady Galliard
marries Sir Charles:

L. GAL., *sighing and looking on Wilding, giving Sir Charles her hand.*
One last look more, and then—be gone fond Love.[72]

"Be gone, fond Love": thus speaks Cupid's idle apprentice
at the end of the fable. To this the kind midnight admittances
and the gloomy bed—indeed a gloomy bed—have brought
her. So also is the loose Mrs. Fainall left at the end of *The Way
of the World*. Her exploration of vice has justified the precepts
of virtue: in particular, the Epicurean maxim that without
practising virtue nobody achieves happiness: "Belinda",
cries the poor, spited, dissolute Mrs. Loveit at the end of
Etherege's *Man of Mode*, 'if thou wouldst be happy, give thyself
wholly up to goodness". Millamant, on the other hand, is
love's industrious apprentice. By winning Mirabell back

to the ways of Caroline honour, she makes their love no mere excrescence of whim and chance, but the lasting affirmation of the traditional decencies; and the union of two minds within a shared culture. Millamant and Mirabell chime with each other like two tuned bells. "*Like Phoebus sung the no less amorous boy*", she murmurs, absently repeating the poetry she delights in. Mirabell, overhearing, wafts in with the other half of the couplet by the Cavalier poet Waller: "*Like Daphne she, as lovely and as coy*. Do you lock yourself up from me, to make my search more curious? Or is this pretty artifice contrived to signify that here the chase must end, and my pursuit be crowned, for you can fly no further?" Enlarged and Baroque they cleave the blue air side by side, like immortals on a polychrome ceiling at Hampton Court, bound not for an illusory Cythera but for a sky where Honour is the sun.

CHAPTER FOUR

I am my Own Fever:
Reason and Impulse in Restoration Comedy

THE FORMS OF a polite society frequently constrain its members to act a part: to disguise impulse in reason, to mask passion and appetite with decorum. The personal reality is often at a remove from the social appearance. "Tell me not," cries Wycherley's Manly at the opening of *The Plain Dealer*, "of your *Decorums*, supercilious forms, and slavish Ceremonies." Manly has just returned from a sea-fight with the Dutch, in which he irascibly scuttled his ship to prevent it from falling into the enemy's hands. "You are too passionate", remarks Lord Plausible. Unlike his friend Freeman, who, a merry and cynical complier with the age, makes much of acquaintances he really despises (declining to "swear against himself" by officiously telling the truth), Manly refuses to "tread round in a preposterous huddle of Ceremony":

> Here you see a *Bishop* bowing low to a gaudy Atheist; a Judge, to a Doorkeeper; a great Lord, to a Fishmonger . . . and so tread round in a preposterous huddle of Ceremony to each other, whilst they can hardly hold Their solemn false countenances.[1]

"Well, they understand the world", replies Freeman. In Freeman's view, telling the truth is a quality "as prejudicial to a man that would thrive, as square play to a cheat, or true love to a whore".

Manly, who has become curt and surly because of his scorn for the artificialities of fashionable life, returns from sea to find that his trusted mistress, Olivia, has stolen his money and secretly married the fop Vernish. Fidelia, who loves Manly, accompanies him disguised as a boy. The character of Manly is derived, in the most general way, from Molière's *Le Misan-thrope*, but the plot is largely *Twelfth Night* brutally brought up to date. As Wycherley says in the prologue to the play:

> But the coarse Dauber of the coming Scenes,
> To follow Life, and Nature only means:
> Displays you, as you are: makes his fine Woman
> A mercenary Jilt, and true to no man;
> His Men of Wit and pleasure of the Age
> Are as dull Rogues as ever cumber'd stage.[2]

Wycherley tears off the masks from "life and nature": instead of the airy fantastic Orsino, there is the truth-telling savage, Manly, whom Wycherley regards as an equally impractical and unworldly figure. Instead of the dreamy Viola, there is the saucy chatterbox Fidelia, who gets into some pretty indelicate scrapes and rescues herself from them with tomboy brio. Instead of Shakespeare's Olivia there is the pretentious blue-stocking of Wycherley.

In Manly's attempt to account for Olivia's betrayal of him Wycherley presents a kind of aghast crudity—the feelings of the ape beneath the measured exterior:

> Her love!—a Whores, a Witches Love!—But, what, did she not kiss well, Sir?—I'm sure I thought her Lips—but I must not think of 'em more—but yet they are such I could still kiss—grow to—and then tear off with my teeth.[3]

As impetuously as he entrusted his money to Olivia, with the same weak judgement, he decides upon his vengeance. He sends Fidelia to Olivia, not to woo her on his behalf, but to decoy her into an assignation where Manly can revenge himself by raping her, plunging vindictively into her truth. Fidelia resists his scheme, appalled not only by its iniquity but also by her own jealousy:

> FIDELIA. But are you sure 'tis Revenge, that makes you do this? how can it be?
> MANLY. Whist!
> FIDELIA. 'Tis a strange Revenge, indeed.[4]

Ardently, and not wholly in a disinterested spirit, she tries to dissuade Manly from his atrocious revenge. As he goes to keep the tryst with Olivia, Fidelia pulls him back: "D'ye call that Revenge? Can you think of such a thing? But reflect, Sir, how she hates and loathes you. . . . No, Sir, no; to be Revenged on her now were to disappoint her. Pray, sir, let us begone."[5]

The fact that, having carried out his purpose whilst Fidelia guards the door, Manly arranges another assignation for the following night, suggests that his "revenge" is only an excuse he makes to himself for his persisting desire for Olivia. In his soliloquy at the beginning of the Third Act, he admits as much. Even with himself he is no plain dealer. Fidelia sits down and weeps—alienated from the man she loves by the disguise which has kept her at his side. But by the end of the play even Manly, who must have been short-sighted, recognises that Fidelia is a woman; and marries her, finding honesty at last in her virgin devotion. Fidelia, although she has concealed her sex and her class, is the plainest dealer in the play. In his stratagem against Olivia, Manly the titular plain dealer shows himself more ruthlessly perfidious than any of the other characters. He is all the more dangerous, in that he pretends to eschew pretences. Beware, warns Bishop Earle, of the counterfeit of a blunt man: "since he is disguised in a humour, that professes not to disguise".[6] Manly's mask—that of the insensate bully whose reputation for plain dealing allows him to tyrannise, scold and threaten—is not an attractive one; but his face is uglier still.

Wycherley's perception both of the social mask and of "the passion panting under" is at its sharpest in a symbolic scene in his *Gentleman Dancing Master*. Gerrard, maddened by the impudence of Hippolita, is nevertheless forced to give her a dancing lesson before three spectators, hiding from them not only his anger with Hippolita but also his incompetence as a dancing-master. The three spectators are her father, whose gullibility is bred of his refusal to recognise his daughter as an object of sexual desire; Mrs. Caution, the prurient and jealous scandal-monger, who sees non-existent breaches of propriety

and is blind to the actual ones; and Hippolita's fiancé, Mr.
Paris, whose tolerance springs from a self-absorbed indifference
to others. Before these, Gerrard, shaking with resentment and
blaspheming under his breath, must smile and make a graceful
leg as he introduces the bow, the step and the skip in their
due proportions. It is one of the best-turned scenes Wycherley
ever wrote.[7] As in Gluck's *Orfeo*, the Furies rampage to a stately
measure. *The Gentleman Dancing Master* may be regarded as
Wycherley's first handling of the principle, stressed in *The
Country Wife*, that vice lies in the intent as well as the deed.
"I never lived so wicked a life", says Hippolita in *The Gentleman
Dancing Master*, "as I have done this twelvemonth, since I
have not seen a man":

> MRS. CAUTION. How, how! if you have not seen a man, how could
>   you be wicked? how could you do any ill?
> HIPPOLITA. No, I have done no ill, but I have paid it with thinking.
> MRS. CAUTION. O that's no hurt!

Hippolita protests that she often dreams naughtily: "and I
am so very scrupulous, that I would as soon consent to a naughty
man as to a naughty dream":

> MRS. CAUTION. I do believe you.
> HIPPOLITA. I am for going into the Throng of Temptations.
> MRS. CAUTION. There I believe you again.
> HIPPOLITA. And making myself so familiar with them, that I
>   would not be concerned for 'em a whit.
> MRS. CAUTION. There I do not believe you.[8]

Horner, who is called "the sign of a man" by Sparkish in
The Country Wife, stands for the moral emasculation of a man in
genteel company. No doubt much of the dialogue in Wycherley's plays was suggested by the wits' conversation at the Cock
Tavern, Chatelain's eating-house, or his other haunts in Covent
Garden. He has recorded the spurious good fellowship of those
intellectual dandies, whose truest satisfaction lay in bettering
each other's epigrams; whose amours were conducted mainly
for the sake of having droll experiences to tell each other
about. They aimed to impress not so much the women as the

other men. Horner, a realist, is not interested in what the other men think. A practical politician, he wants the actuality of sexual success, not the ostentation of it, and says so in the last lines of the play:

> Vain Fopps but court and dress, and keep a puther,
> To pass for Womens men, with one another;
> But he who aims by women to be priz'd,
> First by the men you see must be despis'd.

Only rarely between these cross-purposes of simulation does a blurting earnestness break out, as in Pinchwife's jealousy when the other men are kissing his bride: "Ten thousand ulcers gnaw away their lips. . . . Out of breath and coloured! I must hold yet."[9] Passionate like Manly, a yielder like Manly to aggressive impulses, Pinchwife scuttles his own fortunes like Manly. It is uncomfortably earnest for a comedy.

"Pray, My Lord, don't let the Company see you in this Disorder", Lady Touchwood warns her husband at a tense moment in Congreve's *Double Dealer*.[10] Lady Touchwood herself, like Etherege's Mrs. Loveit and Shadwell's Mrs. Termagant, is a Phaedra in a drawing-room, who fatally abandons herself to her own impulses. Early in the play her lover Maskwell is obliged to tell her not to shout at him so furiously, lest she should be overheard by the company; and Lord Touchwood discovers her infidelity—concealed as he is behind a screen—by hearing another of her infuriated outcries against Maskwell.[11] "You should hate with prudence", Mirabell warns Mrs. Fainall in *The Way of the World*. Lady Touchwood's passion destroys the contrivances of Maskwell's reason. But at first her malice towards Mellefont, her nephew by marriage who has shrunk from her advances, is "like a dark lanthorn" which shines only where it is directed. In society she does Mellefont what harm she can with a "face of kindness"; but alone with him, she melts into tears and is tongue-tied by her feelings. "Words", she says, "are the weak Support of cold Indifference; Love has no Language to be heard."[12] Maskwell's insight into Lady Touchwood's true nature gives him his command over her. "O, Maskwell," she admits, "in vain I do disguise me from thee, thou know'st me, knowest the very inmost Windings and Recesses of my Soul."[13] Whilst plotting Mellefont's downfall, she addresses her heart: "Fall a little thou swelling Heart; let me have some Intermission of this Rage, and one Minute's Coolness to dissemble."[14]

"Women are not the same bare-faced and in masks", says Mellefont's friend, Careless; to which Mellefont replies that women may most properly be said to be unmasked when they wear masks, since then they need not pretend to blush: "and next to being in the Dark, or alone, they are most truly themselves in a Vizor Mask".[15] Lady Touchwood's sister-in-law, Lady Plyant, aims to be artful in her management of the social mask. She deliberately lets it slip when she thinks it expedient to reveal her feelings. "O Lord, what did I say!" she exclaims to Mellefont, having deliberately appraised him of her jealousy of his bride, Cynthia. "I am not safe if I stay," she says to Careless, who is decoying her into decoying her husband; and she stays.[16] The dishonest Lady Froth, whose learned pursuits of poetry and astrology become only a cover for her affair with Mr. Brisk, begins her speeches again and again with "I swear", only to end with "I vow". Dissimulation is very natural to a woman, claims Wycherley's Hippolita, justifying her own pretences: "the mask of simplicity and innocency is as useful to an intriguing woman as the mask of religion to a statesman, they say".[17] "'Tis taking off the ladies' masks," protests Wycherley in the Dedication to *The Plain Dealer*, "not offering at their petticoats, which offends 'em."

Whilst the guileless Lady Plyant simulates a guileful guilelessness, the guileful Maskwell simulates a guileless guilefulness. Maskwell is able to go directly about his treacherous business, since everyone believes that his directness is a stratagem. "No mask like open Truth", he says:

> No Mask like open Truth to cover Lies,
> As to go Naked is the best Disguise.[18]

Thus Lady Froth and Mr. Brisk are able to conceal their inclination towards each other by expressing it openly, but in literary and ceremonious terms, as if it was only a game. They are able to be sincere since nobody suspects them of sincerity: Mr. Brisk, who keeps a looking-glass in the lid of his snuff-box, so that he may adjust his social face, and Lady Froth, well known for her spurious effusiveness to her husband, Lord Froth. Contrasted with these outward shows, the marriage of Cynthia to Mellefont wholly disregards social appearances. They declare for "downright villainous love", and care nothing for the opinion of the world:

> MELLEFONT. Pox o'Fortune, Portion, Settlement and Jointures.
> CYNTHIA. Ay, ay, what have we to do with 'em; you know we marry for Love.
> MELLEFONT. Love, Love, downright very villainous love.
> CYNTHIA. And he that can't live upon Love, deserves to die in a Ditch.[19]

Yet, like Congreve's other honest lovers, Valentine and Angelica, Mirabell and Millamant, they are forced by the insincerities of society to intrigue for their happiness.

In that society even friendship becomes a sort of cunning. "What employment have I for a friend?" exclaims Valentine:

> I am no married Man and thou canst not lye with my Wife! I am very poor, and thou canst not borrow Mony of me.[20]

Pinchwife's maxim in *The Country Wife* is: "He that shows his Wife or Mony, will be in danger of having them borrow'd sometimes"; and certainly Harcourt does not press his friendship upon Sparkish until he has decided to dispossess Sparkish of his wife.

Etherege's Dorimant, in *The Man of Mode*, is at the same time irritated by social artifices and scornful of those who bungle them, whether through intemperance like Mrs. Loveit, or through ineptitude, like Sir Fopling Flutter. He speaks of "tearing off the mask to show the passion that's panting under" in terms which suggest that he likes neither the mask nor the passion. Harriet attracts him because she is captive to neither. She is the drudge neither of social convention nor of any violence in her own feelings: her reason suffers neither external nor internal compulsion. Dorimant's treatment of women other than Harriet is not wholly explicable, even in terms of a cruel enjoyment of power, without taking into account his derision of all sentiment. Like the Earl of Rochester, his supposed original, Dorimant finds the instinctive life—the life of sweat, pulsation and secretion—repellent, and undergoes it only in a mood of melancholy, deliberate debauch. His behaviour towards Mrs. Loveit is practical satire. He lashes in others the weaknesses he shuns in himself.

Aphra Behn's *The Town Fop* (which owes something to *Romeo and Juliet*, although certainly no romanticism) presents the stately family of Lord Plotwell as a microcosm of the *beau monde*. The younger members of the family, driven counter to their own will and sentiment by the stern calculations of the social lawgiver, Lord Plotwell, betray their own hearts and suffer for it. Lord Plotwell tries to sail them against the wind. He wants to breed his family like race-horses, regardless of their own inclinations, and disposing of them in marriage according to his notions of expediency. By the threat of disinheritance he forces his nephew, Bellmour, to marry the rich Lady Diana instead of Celinda, whom Bellmour loves. As a result Bellmour turns savage and abandons himself to a life of hopeless Byronic licence. On his wedding night he asks Sir Timothy Tawdrey to take him to a bawdy house. This is too much for Sir Timothy: "What, already! This is the very quintessence of lewdness."[21] The order so dear to Lord Plotwell breaks down because of his own contrivances. Murder is contemplated as a way of settling the difficulties which the unwise arbiter, like Juliet's father, has created. Friendlove, hoping to marry Lady Diana because "she has a fortune sufficient to excuse her other faults", tries to kill Bellmour in order to please her. Bellmour stabs his own brother Charles, who comes to reclaim him from the brothel:

BELLMOUR. How dar'st thou trust thy self alone with me?
CHARLES. Why should I fear thee?

BELLMOUR. Because I am mad, Mad as a Tygress rob'd of her
    dear Young.
CHARLES. What is't that makes you so?
BELLMOUR. My Uncle's Politicks, Hell take him for't, Has ruin'd
    me, thou and my Sister too.[22]

The distrust of social institutions is still more pronounced in
Shadwell's *A True Widow*. The argument here is a notable one,
since Shadwell resists the fashionable Hobbesian view that the
instincts of Man, necessarily predatory, are curbed rather than
expressed by morality. In France during these years the argument in favour of the natural beneficence of the human heart
was also urged by La Bruyère, in the *Discours* prefaced to his
translation of Theophrastus, and by the convivial Abbé de
Chaulieu.

Shadwell puts forward the view that morality is absolute,
and not merely incidental to a particular society and situation.
The impulses of the heart ardent for goodness and honesty are
to be preferred to the schemes of the mind anxious for gain.
Isabella resists the wishes of her thoroughly corrupt family,
stands out for the virtue innate in her, and, even in worldly
terms, succeeds where her compliant sister fails: the story is
strangely similar to that of Colette's *Gigi*. Lady Cheatly, in
spite of the warning contained in her name, manages to trick
numbers of people out of their money, and plans to sell her
two daughters as mistresses to fashionable gentlemen. The
elder sister, Isabella, denies that in this instance "the young
should submit themselves to the gravity and discretion of the
old":

LADY BUSY. Be not so Forward, all things have two faces—Do
    not look upon the wrong one—go to—You are a fine young
    Lady, and are brought by your Lady Mother to Town, the
    General Mart for Beauty. Well—you would be so settled in the
    World, as to have a certain Fond, whereon you may rely,
    which in Age may secure you from Contempt—Good.
ISABELLA. I hope I shall have enough to keep me honest.
LADY BUSY. Nay, Heaven forbid I should persuade you to be
    dishonest: Vertue is a rare thing, a heavenly thing. But, I say

D

still, be mindful of the main—alas a woman is a solitary, helpless Creature without a man, God knows—good—how may this Man be had in Marriage, say you?—very well—if you could get a fine Gentleman with Money enough; but alas! those do not Marry, they have left it off. The Customes of the World change in all Ages.

ISABELLA. In ours for the worse.

LADY BUSY. Very well said—but yet the wisest must obey 'em as they change.[23]

The younger sister, Gartrude, who, Shadwell describes as "very foolish and whorish", takes her principles all too readily from her mother, and allows herself to be debauched at once, in a preliminary way, by three gentlemen in rapid succession.

First she is debauched by Carlos, who says: "You are so pretty and obliging, there's no resisting you. But will you come and see my lodgings? I have the prettiest French things." Almost alarmed by the readiness with which she agrees, Carlos murmurs to himself: "She is very easy, pray Heaven she is sound."[24] Secondly she is debauched by Selfish, who tells her, "Thou shalt be my Chloris, my Phyllis, Celia, my all", before going to brag about his conquest to the other men.[25] Resembling the sneering lover in Rochester's *Letter from Artemisa in the Town to Chloe in the Country*, Selfish found:

> 'twas dull to love above a day,
> Made his ill-natured jest, and went away.

Thirdly she is debauched by Stanmore who, like Mr. Tattle in Congreve's *Love for Love*, feels the utmost disdain for the mind of the object of his physical appetite: "What an entertainment is this to me that I could love such a thing."[26] As a consequence of her encounters, Gartrude is forced to marry Young Maggot, whom she detests. Young Maggot, the author of *An epigram written in a lady's bible at church*, only undertakes to marry Gartrude because his uncle thinks she has a great deal of money. At the end of the play, Shadwell leaves the newly wed Young Maggot learning that Gartrude is penniless; whilst Gartrude makes an assignation with one of the men who have already hackneyed her in the ways of promiscuity. Meanwhile Isabella steadfastly refuses to become the whore of Bellamour, who admiring her constancy, masters his suspicion of the rite of marriage, and so weds her:

ISABELLA. I'll not deceive you: Whatever show my Mother makes, I have no Portion, nor was ever troubled at the thought of it till now.
BELLAMOUR. I am glad of it; for now my love will be the more easily believed and better taken.[27]

In preferring intuition to an understanding of "the Dirty Devices of this World", Shadwell is in accord with his contemporary, Traherne. Although not, like Traherne, sequestered among brooks and trees, the cockney Shadwell is ready to say, with Traherne, "I knew by Intuition those things which since my Apostasie, I Collected again, by the Highest Reason."[28] The "primitive and innocent clarity" of Isabella's first light has not been blown out by the customs and manners of the adult world. More than thirty years before the publication of the *Characteristics*, Shadwell, drawing upon the same Platonic tradition as Shaftesbury, anticipates Shaftesbury's deliberations upon the implicit goodness of the human heart and the benevolence of its instincts. Whereas Hobbes, who thought all men by nature wolves to all other men, had stressed the need for an absolute social authority to keep the peace, Shadwell, who considered mankind inherently virtuous but vitiated by society, dissented from Hobbes's widely accepted view and found more good in private impulse than in public expediency. All the heroes and heroines of Shadwell's plays seek to escape from society into a life defined by themselves:

There certainly that freedom we must find,
Which is deny'd to us among Mankind.[29]

With this sentiment (taken from Molière's *Le Misanthrope*) Shadwell's first play concludes, and with this sentiment Wycherley brings his last to an end; when the Plain Dealer retires from the world, having regained in the natural and spontaneous Fidelia what he has been cheated of by the artifices of Olivia. The play finishes well for Manly, better than he deserves. By making his impulses his law, and deeming other people only the appurtenances of his own rash will, this ship-scuttler has tried hard, in his spleen, to destroy himself. He has opened himself to every exploitation. But *The Plain Dealer* is a comedy, of sorts. Coriolanus is not broken by his arrogance, but subsists.

Reason is defensive. Mirabell, in his courtship of Millamant, speaks of himself as one of those who are "made wise from the distastes of Reason, and yet persevere to play the fool by the force of instinct". The predators of Restoration Comedy are quick to fall upon such creatures of passion as Manly; for the impulsive person is the natural victim of the maliciously reasonable. Quantities of widows and doting husbands, in particular, are marked down and ambushed as they go upon their avid and heedless ways. With what squawks Lady Wishfort rises as Foible beats the convert for the sharp-shooter Mirabell:

Audacious Villain! handle me, wou'd he durst—Frippery? old Frippery! Was there ever such a foul-mouth'd Fellow? I'll be marry'd to Morrow, I'll be contracted to Night.[30]

The velocity of her own emotions drives her in the direction Mirabell wishes her to take. In Etherege's *The Comical Revenge*, Sir Frederick Frollick coarsely woos a widow more forbearing than Lady Wishfort, but equally impetuous. They are fellow guests at a wedding. "Ho, widow!" blunt Sir Frederick remarks, "the noise of these Nuptials brought you hither; I perceive your mouth waters."[31] He advances upon the melting creature, none too graciously, as a matter of principle. Her deliquescence shall be profitable to Sir Frederick!

His opinion is this: "Some women, like Fishes, despise the Bait or else suspect it, whilst still it's bobbing at their mouths; but subtilly wav'd by the Angler's hand, greedily hang themselves upon the hook. There are many so critically wise, they'll suffer none to deceive them but themselves."[32] Sir Frederick subtly waves his bait by ringing a hand-bell outside the widow's window at night. "Rise out of bed", he chants:

> Rise out of Bed, and ope the door;
> Here's that will all your joys restore.[33]

The maid comes to the window:

> MAID. Who's that that comes at this unseasonable hour, to disturb my Ladies quiet?
> SIR FREDERICK. An honest Bell-man, to mind her of her frailty.

Not discomfitted by the widow's justified annoyance, he departs with the words: "Farewell, widow; I pity thy solitary condition." In spite of such behaviour, the widow agrees to marry him: "Now I have received you into my Family, I hope you will let my maids go quietly about their business, Sir."[34] Sir Frederick, the impassive disposer of the more tender-hearted, virtuously marries off his concubine to Sir Nicholas Cully: "And, give her her due, faith she was a very honest Wench to me, and I believe will make a very honest Wife to you."[35] Lady Wishfort and the newly wed Lady Frollick, those two exemplars of the frailty of widows in Restoration Comedy, can well say, with Wycherley's Widow Flippant: "'Tis well known no Woman breathing could use more industry to get her a Husband that I have."[36]

Akin to these widows in their mindless abandon are the infatuated husbands of Restoration Comedy. In Shadwell's *Epsom Wells* Mr. Bisket, "a humble, civil cuckold", totally subjugated by his wife, longs to be like Mr. Fribble, "a surly cuckold", who keeps his in at least outward good order. Mr. Bisket's failure to manage his wife springs from his doting tenderness for her:

> Oh that I could govern my Wife thus! if I thought I could, I would swinge my Duck extreamly, I'd beat my Lamb inordinately.[37]

The citizens' use in public of nicknames and expressions of affection was something repeatedly condemned by the leaders of fashion at the time. Millamant makes it one of the conditions of her marrying Mirabell that he shall never "call her names" in public:

> Ay, as Wife, Spouse, my Dear, Joy, Jewell, Love Sweet-heart, and the rest of that nauseous Cant, in which Men and their Wives are so fulsomly familiar,—I shall never bear that.[38]

Aphra Behn's *Sir Patient Fancy* should be considered as a study of reason relinquished to uxorious passion. At first sight, the plot is a cruel one. Sir Patient is a hypochondriac, like Molière's Argan; but his mental sufferings are more pitiful than comical. His young wife's betrayal of his trust, by encouraging his morbid fancies, cuckolding him, and stealing his money, is distinctly unamusing. Lady Fancy is a narcissist luxuriating in the charms of her own body. She speaks of her husband's doting love: "He does the office of my women, dresses and undresses me, and does so smirk at his handiwork."[39] With a trace of indulgence she mocks her husband's Puritan companions, who "do so sneer at me, pat my breasts and cry fie, fie upon this fashion of tempting nakedness".[40] Sir Patient is the opposite of the gallants who frequented the playhouses. He claims to "do nothing without reason and precaution", in spite of being so besotted by Lady Fancy, and speaks of "the good days of the late Protector".[41]

Lady Fancy has a disreputable past. Her maid, admitting Lady Fancy's lover in the dark, says:

> Now I am return'd to my old Trade again, fetch and carry my Lady's Lovers; I was afraid when she had been married, these Night-works would have ended.[42]

But, perhaps because she is out of practice, the maid brings the wrong lover to Lady Fancy, Lodwick instead of Wittmore:

> MAID. I see you'se a punctual Lover, Sir pray follow me as softly as you can.

LODWICK. This is someone who I perceive *Isabella* has made the Confident to our Amours.[43]

For Lodwick is in love with Isabella, Lady Fancy's step-daughter. In the dark he mistakes Lady Fancy for Isabella, whilst Lady Fancy thinks Lodwick is Wittmore:

LADY FANCY. Oh the agreeable Confusion of a Lover high with expectation of the approaching Bliss! What tremblings between Joy and Fear possess me?

Lodwick is horrified by the apparent lascivious forwardness of the girl he intends to marry, and expresses his dismay; in answer to which Lady Fancy, deceived in her own deceit, exclaims:

What ails you? are you mad?—we are safe, and free as Winds let loose to ruffle all the Groves; what is't delays you then? Soft.

"Pox of this thought of Wife," Lodwick says to himself, "the very Name destroys my appetite". Then Lady Fancy alludes to her husband. Lodwick at last realises the mistake, but is rascal enough to take advantage of it. Later in the play the moral intention becomes plainer. It is shown that Sir Patient needed to discover the looseness and perfidy of his wife in order to recover his health, dismiss the doctors who had done him so much harm, and regain his intellectual balance.

The pretence of lisping babyish simplicity put on by Mrs. Laetitia Fondlewife, in Congreve's *The Old Bachelor*, makes her deceit of Mr. Fondlewife seem viler still. In Fondlewife's absence, Bellmour disguised as Vainlove-disguised-as-a-priest keeps an assignation with Mrs. Fondlewife. Vainlove is a male flirt who cannot bear to proceed with a woman once she has capitulated to him, so passes his conquests on to Bellmour, who has a less exacting taste, and more appetite. Mrs. Fondle-wife soon discovers that Bellmour has taken Vainlove's place, but, not being very discriminating, decides Bellmour to be an acceptable makeshift. Their unsentimental transaction com-pleted, they are surprised by Fondlewife's return. Bellmour admits that he intended to seduce Mrs. Fondlewife, but pretends to Fondlewife that he did not succeed; and the pitiful Fondlewife is easily persuaded to believe what he longs to believe.

The scene ends with a couplet in which Bellmour expresses the subjectivity of love, a theme which is renewed in the adventures of Heartwell, the old bachelor himself:

> No Husband, by his Wife can be deceiv'd;
> She still is vertuous if she's so believ'd.[44]

Fondlewife, unlike Wycherley's Pinchwife, is an inoffensive person. A favourite locution with Congreve is "Pardon me, my dear creature, I must laugh", followed by a particularly mirthless laugh. This recalls the lines of Congreve's master, Juvenal, who laughed at the serious concerns of the mob, and also at its pleasures, although he sometimes dropped a tear for all his merriment.[45] Our compassion for Fondlewife certainly prevents us from finding his betrayal funny. The pathos of his predicament lies beyond the bounds of comedy. In a way, Congreve's morality is more traditional than that of Wycherley, who does, after all, in *The Country Wife*, suggest that adultery is condonable in certain situations: Congreve's disgust with Mrs. Fondlewife is utter. Congreve presents the episode more as a warning rather than as an example. Reasoning with himself, Fondlewife admits that Mrs. Fondlewife is young and vigorous, and he old and impotent:

> Then why didst thee marry, Isaac?—Because she was beautiful and tempting, and because I was obstinate and doating.

Belinda's remark, in the same play, may be taken as an apt comment on Fondlewife and Heartwell: "This Love is the devil, and sure to be in love is to be possessed."

Heartwell, the middle-aged and misanthropic bachelor after whom this play is named, professes to despise women and "Dressing, Dancing, Singing, Sighing, Whining, Rhyming, Flattering, Lying, Grinning, Cringing, and the drudgery of Loving to boot."[46] But not having been inoculated, by a varied experience of women, against the wiles of the dishonest ones, he is smitten by Vainlove's discarded mistress, Silvia. In a scene of great dramatic irony Congreve enunciates the subjectivity of love (deceiving the lover in himself and laying him open to deceit from outside) by making Heartwell desire Silvia for the qualities she least has. Heartwell, like Fondlewife, is all too willing to be persuaded to propagate his illusion.

In the same sentence Heartwell calls her angel and devil, saint and witch, since in his confused inward life it is possible for her to be both. He perceives only his own sensations. He reproaches himself for gazing at her, yet says that he must, whilst for her part she tells him not to stare so. "O Dotage!" he exclaims, "that ever that noble Passion, Lust, should ebb to this degree." Her appearance of innocence, which at once torments and pleases him, stirs him to arguments against his own determination not to marry her; so that, when she turns to go from him, he cheats his own will by calling her back. He offers her a parting kiss. With that kiss, his reason capitulates to his impulse:

> HEARTWELL. By Heav'n her kiss is sweeter than Liberty—I will marry thee—There thou hast don't. All my Resolves melted in that Kiss—one more.
> SILVIA. But when?
> HEARTWELL. I'm impatient 'till it be done; I will not give my self Liberty to think, lest I should cool—I will about a Licence straight—in the Evening expect me—One Kiss more to confirm me Mad; so.
> SILVIA. Ha, ha, ha, an old Fox trapt—.[47]

Heartwell himself holds up the mask which prevents him from seeing Silvia's true face. The reality of the object of his passion is as obscure to him as the reality of Sir Samuel Hearty is to Sir Formal Trifle when, in Shadwell's *The Virtuoso*, they are dropped into a cellar together. Sir Formal can think of nothing better to do than to seduce Sir Samuel, who is disguised as a gypsy-woman. Very decorously, and without revealing his disguise, Sir Samuel preserves the honour of his assumed identity. "Come, my dear nymph, let us be more familiar", says Sir Formal. "The solitary darknesss of the place invites us to love's silent pleasures. Now, dearest Chloris, let us taste those sweets." But Sir Samuel will have none of it:

SIR SAMUEL. I am an honest woman, I scorn your words. I will call out for somebody to protect my honour.

SIR FORMAL. Your Honour cannot suffer; none can see us, and who will declare it?

SIR SAMUEL. Out upon you! Get you gone, you swine.

At last, Sir Formal becomes so pressing that Sir Samuel is obliged to fling him to the ground: "Out lustful Tarquin! You libidinous goat, have at you!"[48] In this farcical scene Sir Formal is literally in the dark. As a result of his indifference to anything but his passionate needs and desires, Heartwell too is in a "solitary darkness".

The theme of Congreve's *The Double Dealer*—that one is deceived by oneself more often than by others—is stated in Maskwell's soliloquy at the end of the Second Act: the honest man cheats himself; the wise man is fooled by himself. Hence the hero, Mellefont, sedulously secures himself against the guile of all his enemies except the most vicious of them, Maskwell, whom Mellefont is convinced he has attached to his own dear person. Hence Lady Touchwood fancies she is angry with her lover, Maskwell, because he has helped her to betray her husband; whilst she is really angry because Maskwell has not succeeded in breaking off the match between Cynthia and Mellefont. As Maskwell perceives, she loves Mellefont whilst professing hatred for him and plotting his ruin. Lady Touchwood also deludes herself by believing that she obliges Maskwell by subjecting her person, as she calls it, to his pleasure. On the contrary, Maskwell, glutted with her, dreads the approaching coition, and the raptures which he must dissemble. Lady Plyant's conceit goes further. She is so sure that Mellefont loves her that she takes his shocked denials as confirmation of his love.

Five of the characters in *The Double Dealer* deal double with themselves. They do so because of their enamoured and subjective interpretation of others. Only Maskwell, the villain, does not trick himself—does not sponsor his own illusions. The burden of *The Double Dealer*, as of *The Old Bachelor*, though voiced not without gaiety, is that of the Chevalier de Parny:

> Que les serments sont un mensonge,
> Que l'amour trompe tôt ou tard,
> Que l'innocence n'est qu'un art,
> Et que le bonheur n'est qu'un songe.[49]

Lady Touchwood, who rightly describes herself as having fire in her temper, and passions in her soul, apt to every provocation—oppressed as she is with love and with despair—is readily tricked by Maskwell, "a sedate, a thinking Villain, whose black Blood runs temperately bad".[50] Maskwell is a kind of polite Iago, availing himself only of the foolishness latent in his instruments. The foolish rattling Mr. Brisk, a preliminary sketch for Tattle in *Love for Love*, although a witless enough being, is yet able to defraud both Lord and Lady Froth, who are among his few admirers. Ungrateful for Lord Froth's patronage, Brisk makes love to Lady Froth: "The Deuce take me, I can't help laughing my self, ha, ha; yet by Heav'ns I have a violent Passion for your Ladyship, seriously."[51] Lady Plyant, the young wife of the uxorious old knight, Sir Paul Plyant, has "a large Eye, and wou'd centre every Thing in her own Circle; 'tis not the first time she has mistaken Respect for Love, and made Sir Paul jealous of the Civility of an under-signing Person".[52] With Mr. Careless she deceives her husband and herself. As the hero of the play observes, "She's handsome, and knows it; is very silly, and thinks she has Sense, and has an old fond Husband."[53] Lord Touchwood himself, the wise arbiter of the play, is misled again and again by the view of his wife which best satisfies his vanity. He will "be made a Fool of by no Body, but himself".[54] Even Maskwell, in pursuit of his frustrated self-interest, is forced into complaisances with Lady Touchwood for which he has little stomach:

> She has a damn'd penetrating Head, and knows how to interpret
> a Coldness the right Way; therefore I must dissemble ardour and
> Ecstasie, that's resolved: How easily and pleasantly is that
> dissembled before Fruition! Pox on't that a man can't drink
> without quenching his Thirst.[55]

Although such subsidiaries as Lord and Lady Froth are
notional figures to the degree that it is impossible to feel more
concerned over their affairs than over the hazards of Pantaloon
and Columbine in the Commedia dell' Arte, the main plot of
the play, which concerns Lady Touchwood's passion for her
nephew by marriage, is unusually intense for a Restoration
Comedy. She uses as her agent the subtle Maskwell, who carries
the comedy of appearances to its extreme by pretending to
be pretending. Coolness is a defence in the Hobbesian war.
At the best it balks the opponent; at the worst it diminishes his
triumph. "The coldness of a losing Gamester lessens the
pleasure of the Winner", Fainall tells Mirabell at the beginning
of *The Way of the World*, all unaware of what his own lack of
coolness will later cost him. Like other abandoned women in
Restoration Comedy, Lady Touchwood is betrayed by her own
tempestuous nature. Learning of Maskwell's treachery, she
tries to stab him, then weeps:

> But thus my Anger melts. Here, take this Ponyard, for my very
> Spirits faint, and I want Strength to hold it, thou hast disarm'd
> my Soul.[56]

Meanwhile her nephew, Mellefont, has extricated himself from
a plot by which he was, in the hope of tricking Lady Touchwood, tricked into keeping an assignation the purpose of which
is to trick Lord Touchwood. Mr. Brisk's comment, at the end
of *The Double Dealer*, is apt: "This is all very surprising, let
me perish."

The plot of *The Double Dealer* is, indeed, specious. As Congreve
disarmingly says in the Dedication, "I design'd the Moral
first, and to that Moral I invented the Fable." The main
action, possibly touched by a ripple from Racine's recent

Phèdre, is unusually ambitious for a Restoration Comedy. Congreve lacked that utter discretion which kept such writers as Jane Austen so tactfully within their artistic limitations, and in *The Double Dealer* he aspires towards the grandiose effects of his tragedy, *The Mourning Bride*. Yet for all the pat surprises and the banal shifts and reversals of the plot, *The Double Dealer* remains psychologically deft.

In Congreve's view, every event is vitiated by the sensibility which encounters it; so that one spends one's life like Heartwell, nourishing an illusion of experience, and again and again witnessing only oneself:

> Man will admire, adore and die
> While wishing at your feet they lye
> But admitting their Embraces
> Wakes 'em from the Golden Dream;
> Nothing's new beside our Faces,
> Every Women is the same.[57]

Thus love tends always to an egocentric notion of the world, since the lover relates the loved one's conduct only to the lover, so finding all sorts of relevances not truly present:

> I attempt from Loves Sickness to fly in vaine
> Since I am my Self my own feaver and Pain.[58]

The mercury of feeling, instead of telling one what the temperature is outside, too often stays in its little sphere, registering nothing but itself. Lady Touchwood thinks she has found Maskwell in Mellefont and Mellefont in Maskwell. The apparent recurrence of the same object in a succession of objects of desire, as she discovers, is no more than a community in one's own perceptions; so that one perpetuates each experience beyond the point at which it concluded: as the image left behind on closed eyes by a strong light is continued, although ever fugitive and lessening: a deception in retreat.

CHAPTER FIVE

My Heart is the Pendulum:
Epicureanism in Restoration Comedy

THE FIRST COMPLETE English version of Lucretius, by Thomas
Creech, was published in 1682. It appeared on the scene, like
another Millamant, decked out in poetic tributes. Creech, then
only twenty-three, was loaded with the commendations of the
great, from Dryden to Aphra Behn. Dryden advised the reader
who found obscurities in his own translations from Lucretius
to refer to Creech's notes on that author: "which I have often
read, and always with some new pleasure".[1] All these commendations Creech, with no excess of modesty, printed at the
beginning of his translation. Every Tory poet turned some
gentlemanly couplets to welcome it—and what poet of consequence was not a Tory, apart from Shadwell, whom the Tory
poets claimed was so perpetually foxed with claret that his
views did not matter? Creech was surrounded by a murmura-
tion of complimentary verses. There in his *Lucretius*, in the
philosophy of the age of Cicero, was found the testament of
Mirabell and Dorimant: affirmation of moral individualism,
subject only to a freely exercised reason; affirmation of the
beneficence of Pleasure; affirmation also of the philosophical
merit which lies in searching out, like the Royal Society,
the physical causes of things; affirmation, even, of a post-
Cromwellian irreligion. After Creech's translation it became
all the more difficult for a man of wit and sense to believe
in, and tremble at, Hell, except as a state of mind:

> But that which senseless we so grossly fear,
> No Hell, no sul'phrous Lakes, no Pools appear.[2]

The ancient Cavalier poet, Edmund Waller, was astonished
at the "wondrous fire of the young translator".

> Pardon this Rapture, Sir, but who can be
> Cold and unmov'd, yet have his Thoughts on Thee?[3]

John Evelyn, who had earlier translated part of Lucretius, ceded to Creech whatever territorial rights he had acquired by that pioneering work. Evelyn made the discovery, but was too weak and poor to turn it to a conquest:

> Columbus thus, only discover'd Land,
> But it was won by great Corteze's Hand.[4]

Creech has subdued the land of Epicurus, and by just title deserves its crown.

Nahum Tate extolled Creech's footnotes, which record the moral errors of Lucretius and provide an antidote for his poison:

> From Epicurus' Walks thus weeding Vice,
> No more the Garden, but a Paradise.[5]

Thomas Otway, urging Creech to translate Virgil next, decried the scribblers of the age:

> Go on in pity to this wretched Isle,
> Which ignorant Poetasters thus defile,
> With lousy Madrigals for Lyric Verse;
> Instead of Comedy with nasty Farce.[6]

Aphra Behn did Creech the honour of melting for him, as for so many others:

> Whilst that, which Admiration does inspire
> In other Souls, kindles in mine a Fire.[7]

Feminist as ever, she thanked Creech for giving her sex access to a text originally written in a language from which masculine prejudice had excluded them. Until Creech translated Lucretius, Aphra Behn had cursed the stinting customs of her country, which did not permit women to read such "learned Heroes dead" as Homer and "the Godlike Virgil":

> We are forbid all grateful Themes,
> No ravishing Thoughts approach our Ear;
> The fulsome Gingle of the Times
> Is all we are allowed to understand or hear.

But now her grievance was in some measure redressed by Creech's Lucretius. She paraphrased Horace's lines about the poet as the first civiliser of men:

> Gentler they grew, their Words and Manners chang'd;
> And Savage now no more the Woods they rang'd;
> So Thou by this Translation dost advance
> And equall'st Us to Man.[8]

Aphra Behn's lover, John Hoyle, she told Creech in a later verse-letter, was:

> A Wit uncommon, and facetious,
> A great Admirer of Lucretius.[9]

Of the freedom of the will Walter Charleton had already written in *Epicurus's Morals*, published in 1656:

That this arbitrary freedom of our will is the congenial prerogative of our nature is demonstrated unto us not only by our own experience, but also by common sense; which manifesteth that nothing is worthy of praise or blame, but what is done freely, voluntarily, deliberately, and of election; and must therefore depend upon something within us, which is above all compulsion, superintendency, command or controlment.[10]

The comic dramatists of the Restoration found great charm in this Epicurean view that Man is the artificer of his own clay: that his nature is shaped according to his own will, his purpose decided by himself, his life arranged as he thinks best; he himself resisting, by a cool formality, any threat to the perfect self-possession by which he engages voluntarily in a temperate and detached sensuality. That virtue is the necessary attribute of a life of pleasure they did not find so convincing. Sometimes their model of Epicurean conduct was not Epicurus himself, or Lucretius, but Petronius; Petronius, whom a French writer of the time, Jean François Sarasin, summed up as a professional voluptuary.[11] Epicurus was taken to be, in the words of the Seigneur de Saint-Évremond, "a sensual and lazy person, that never quitted his idleness but to make a debauch".[12] Here they were in error, as a brief consideration of Epicurean philosophy will show.

To the educated classes of Ancient Rome, as early as in the republican period to which Lucretius belonged, the half-savage old gods of the Greeks—licentious Jupiter, Apollo with his fierce arrows of pestilence, Dis and his dog with its three heads grinning—had become little more than figures of poetic romance and vehicles for the ceremonial of the state. Their rites were performed exactly and with inward scepticism. They were propitiated and disregarded. Few earnestly believed in them, but fewer denied them; for the Romans were sternly conservative. To have denied the Gods would have been indecorous, and disrespectful to the pieties of a former age. Conservatism took the place of belief, but conservatism itself incorporated a form of worship of the Gods. In their temples the satisfaction or dismay of the state was registered.

Most Roman patricians of the time of Cicero who gave any thought at all to religious questions were adherents to one or the other of the two schools of philosophy which were founded in Athens not long after the death of Aristotle: Stoicism and Epicureanism. The two schools, both of which derived some of their notions from Plato, had more in common than is often supposed. Neither had a fixed body of doctrine, and each borrowed from the other. The Stoics, in particular, shifted their ground several times. At first they had believed in a life after death, but by the time of Lucretius had come to doubt it; and the Stoic Seneca paraphrases from Lucretius, in a passage translated into English by the Earl of Rochester, the Epicurean refutation of the immortality of the soul. On the other hand, Lucretius, who denies all supernatural causes, inconsistently—perhaps for the sake of a Roman respectability—concedes the existence of the Gods; although with the reservation that they take no part in human affairs.

Whilst the Epicureans were in effect atheists, the Stoics were theists, regarding God (as Plato does in his *Symposium*) as the activating principle of the material Universe. According to the Stoics, there is an eternally renewed cycle of history in which everything goes from good to bad and ends in flames—in a *Götterdämmerung*: hence their longing for the beatitudes of a rural past, for an illusory Golden Age as in Juvenal, or a subjectively envisaged Germania as in Tacitus. The Epicureans, on the contrary, thought that Man progesses continuously from a primitive and benighted into a more and more enlightened condition, as in Lucretius's account of the history of Early Man in Book V of *De Rerum Natura*.[13]

In their ethics the Stoics and the Epicureans differed less. Their principles were the same. They diverged only temperamentally, and in the placing of emphasis here or there. They agreed that the man who is happy or unhappy according to his good or bad fortune renders himself the slave of chance; that, therefore, he must harden himself against his circumstances by the exercise of his will: not to be the creature of his emotions, but to choose freely after rational consideration. The Stoics tried to liberate the will through abstinence and endurance, the Epicureans through impassivity and understanding. (Horner is Wycherley's Epicurean, whereas Manly, in his thwarting of his own emotion and his resentment of pleasure, is Wycherley's Stoic.) Thus, whilst the Stoics despised the natural sciences, the Epicureans regarded the natural sciences as instruments for knowing the causes they were at issue with. Lucretius regarded the fear of the Gods and the fear of death as the dominating reasons for human misery; attempting to assuage both fears by his explanation of the nature of things. As Dryden puts it, in his free translation of the Epicurean Second Georgic of Virgil:

> Happy the Man, who, studying Nature's Laws,
> Through known Effects can trace the secret Cause:
> His Mind possessing, in a quiet state,
> Fearless of Fortune, and resign'd to Fate.[14]

For this reason, the bent of the Stoics was active, whilst that of the Epicureans was scholarly and contemplative. The Stoics gathered in the market-place whilst the Epicureans withdrew to their gardens, deeming happiness to be, in the words of Epicurus, "the repose of the body and the tranquillity of the mind".[15] Both Stoics and Epicureans held the practice of virtue to be the chief good, but virtue to the Stoics consisted largely of traditional *pietas*: observances enforced by duty. Cato was cruel to his slaves; Seneca excused the atrocities of his pupil Nero; Marcus Aurelius watched the pitiless spectacles of the Roman arena. Virtue was a more utilitarian thing to the Epicureans, and a necessary consequence of the prudence, moderation and fortitude without which a life of rational pleasure would be impossible. But neither Stoics nor Epicureans suggested that there was any supernatural sanction for the practice of virtue.[16]

Of the works of Epicurus himself only some lengthy fragments survive, preserved chiefly in a biography written by Diogenes Laertius in the third century A.D. Epicurus's philosophy was tersely summed up by one of his disciples, Diogenes of Oenoanda: "There is nothing to fear from the Gods and nothing to fear after death. Good can be attained and evil endured". As a scientist Epicurus was less impressive than as a moral philosopher. He regards the Universe as a fortuitous motion of occasionally conglomerating atoms—"the foppish casual dance of atoms", as his seventeenth-century translator, Walter Charleton, calls it.[17] More important are his propositions, which can be regarded as distinct from his metaphysics, on the subject of right conduct, and his arguments against the immortality of the soul. At least his scientific enquiries initiated a search for natural laws. Although he mistook the laws, at least he recognised that laws existed.

Because of the power and imagination of his expression, and because the three hundred scrolls of Epicurus's writings have been lost, Lucretius has become the chief spokesman for the Epicurean philosophy. Books I and II and VI of Lucretius's *De Rerum Natura* are chiefly devoted to the theory of the atoms. The central Books, from which Dryden made extensive translations—Book III, on the folly of fearing death, and Book

IV, on the nature of sensation and sexual desire—were the ones of most interest to the writers of the Restoration.

Whilst he concedes that the Gods (whom perhaps he thinks of as Platonic abstractions) exist, Lucretius denies that they trouble themselves about the behaviour or the fate of mortals. Creech translates the lines thus:

> For ev'ry Deity must live in Peace,
> In undisturb'd and everlasting Ease:
> Nor care for us, from Fears and Dangers free:
> Sufficient to his own Felicity:
> Nought here below, Nought in our Pow'r he needs;
> Ne'er smiles at good, ne'er frowns at wicked Deeds.[18]

To these lines a footnote, apparently not by Creech himself, is added:

> The Gods lie supinely indulging themselves in Indolence, and lulled in undisturbed Repose: they take no Care of the Affairs of the Earth, and are wholly unconcerned at the good or ill Actions of Men. . . . Behold the true Image of the Epicurean God! How thoughtless and supine he lies, indulging himself in Ease and Idleness.

The same lines were curtly and forcefully translated by Rochester, who for his part lets them pass without reproach.[19]

In the passage which follows, which Hobbes must have had in mind when he wrote his account of the progress of superstition in *Leviathan*, Lucretius dismisses as a silly fancy the notion that there is a god of the sea, or a god of wine, or a Mother Goddess called Cybele.[20] Names such as Bacchus and Ceres, he says, should be used only figuratively. Having shown the fear of the Gods to be unreasonable, Lucretius goes on, in Book III, to demonstrate by twenty-eight arguments that it is equally unreasonable to fear death: "Therefore Death is nothing to us, nor does it in the least concern us." He personifies Nature, who tells Mankind: "Although you should outlive all ages, you would still find nothing you have not already known. Everything is always the same".[21] Dryden has translated Nature's speech:

Why dost thou not give Thanks, as at a plenteous Feast,
Cramb'd to the Throat with Life, and rise, and take thy Rest?
But if my Blessings thou has thrown away;
If undigested Joys pass'd through, and would not stay;
Why dost thou wish for more to squander still?
If Life be grown a Load, a real Ill,
And I would all thy Cares and Labours end;
Lay down thy Burden, Fool, and know thy friend:
To please thee, I have empty'd all my Store,
I can invent, and can supply no more;
But run the Round again, the Round I ran before.[22]

Eadem sunt omnia semper: that is exactly the sentiment of Etherege's characters at the beginning of *She Would If She Could*; of Sir John Brute at the beginning of *The Provoked Wife*; of Dryden's own Rhodophil and Palamede at the beginning of *Marriage à la Mode*.

Since there is no life after death, Lucretius continues, it follows that the only Hell is the Hell which fools make for themselves on Earth: fools, and those troubled in conscience for their misdeeds. It is here or nowhere that Tantalus, that Tityos, that Sisyphus suffers. The grim dog of Hell, the Furies, and the alienation from the light, are no more than guilt, and the present fear of retribution for evil done:

> The Furies, *Cerberus*, black Hell, and Flames,
> Are airy Fansies all, meer empty Names.[23]

Dryden's translation of the passage is even more spirited than the original:

> As for the Dog, the Furies, and their Snakes,
> The gloomy Caverns, and the burning Lakes,
> And all the vain infernal Trumpery,
> They neither are, nor were, nor e'er can be.[24]

Epicureanism had little effect upon English Literature until the seventeenth century, and at first the effect had been diffused and general. It was only in the controversy which included the publication of Hobbes's *Leviathan* in 1651 that the effect became particular and measurable: in the debate between scepticism and religious belief. Orthodox Christian writers from the beginning of the controversy accused Epicurus and Lucretius of atheism—as if they would have been better pleased if Epicurus and Lucretius had believed in Neptune, Bacchus and Ceres. "Though Epicurus and Democritus babbled something of a deity," wrote Alexander Ross in his *Medicus Medicatus* of 1645, "yet in holding the world to be actually and rashly agglomerated of small atoms, they were very atheists."

Hobbes was a cautious and even timorous author; but his *Leviathan* makes it plain that he believes neither in Providence nor in supernatural sanctions for Man's conduct. God and Providence, excluded from his moral system, are replaced by the Right of Nature. This Epicurean concept Hobbes defines as "the Liberty each man hath, to use his power, as he will himselfe, for the preservation of his own Nature; that is to say, of his own Life; and consequently, of doing anything, which in his own Judgement, and Reason, hee shall conceive to be the aptest means thereunto".[25] But the Right of Nature, he adds, exists only in a state of Nature, which he follows the Epicureans in considering to be a poor thing compared with a state of civilisation. Thus men form combinations, and entrust their Right of Nature to the society which they have established for the common benefit. That society determines the character of moral obligation. Wisely, Hobbes avoided metaphysical arguments: he was in enough trouble already. As his friend, John Aubrey, says, a motion was made to burn the good old man as a heretic.

A year after the publication of *Leviathan*, Walter Charleton, a personal friend of Hobbes but his philosophical opponent, returned to the subject of the atoms in his *Darkness of Atheism Discovered*, alluding haughtily to their "foppish casual dance". Charleton reprehends the Epicureans for "plotting to undermine the received belief of an omnipotent eternal being, to murder the immortality of the soul (the basis of all religion) and to deride the compensations of good and evil actions after death".[26] The freethinkers of the Restoration agreed with Charleton, but applauded the Epicurean philosophers for their subversion. In seeking to answer Epicurus's arguments, Charleton was in some measure convinced by them. In 1654 he ventured an explanation of Epicurean physics under the quaint title of *Physiologia Epicuro-Gassendo-Charletoniana*. Far from exhausted by the ardours of the *Physiologia Epicuro-Gassendo-Charletoniana*, Charleton went on to justify Epicurus's moral thought in *Epicurus's Morals*, published in 1656. Although this book is of the greatest historical importance, as representing Epicurus as he was known to Dryden and his contemporaries, it is not a trustworthy version of Epicurus's own writings as preserved by Diogenes Laertius but a scagliola of fragments from Epicurus, Lucretius, Cicero, Seneca and Marcus Aurelius, with no indication of the sources.

At Oxford when *Epicurus's Morals* was published were two young men who were later to represent the two ends of the scale of Restoration Literature: the postgraduate Thomas Traherne and the undergraduate Earl of Rochester. It is likely that such a book, at such a time in their lives, would have come to their notice. Each according to his own bent would have found what he was looking for in Epicureanism. For Rochester it was an irreligious free-will; for Traherne it was Felicity.

There are two kinds of pleasure, writes Charleton. One is "radicated in Quiet" and is "a constant placability, calmness, and vacuity or immunity from all perturbation and dolour". The other, which arises from "a pleasant motion in the organs", may be considered "resident in motion" and consists of "a certain sweet affectation, or pleasant titillation of the sense". Felicity can consist only in the first kind of pleasure, and "can be no other than the indolency of body and tranquillity of mind".[27] Traherne takes the same view:

When I came into the Country, and being seated among silent Trees, had all my Time in mine own Hands, I resolved to Spend it all, whatever it cost me, in Search of Happiness, and to Satiat that burning Thirst which Nature had Enkindled, in me from my youth. In which I was so resolut, that I chose rather to liv upon 10 pounds a year, and to go in Lether clothes, and feed upon Bread

and Water, so that I might hav all my Time clearly to myself:
then to keep many thousands per Annum in an Estate of Life
where my Time would be Devoured in Care and Labor.[28]

An English translation of Lucretius, Evelyn's rendering of
Book I, was first published in 1656, the same year as Charleton's
Epicurus; although there had been previous unpublished
translations. The fastidious Evelyn, discouraged by the poor
printing of the First Book, desisted from publishing any more.
Evelyn defended Lucretius from his calumniators in an essay
prefixed to the translation. Lucretius, says Evelyn, is no more
irreligious and profane than is to be expected in any heathen
author; and throughout his poem Lucretius "persuades to a
life the most exact and moral".[29] Thomas Stanley's popular
History of Philosophy (1655–61) included a long section on
Epicurus, with translations from Lucretius. With that history,
the Restoration was at hand.

In 1662 the court of Charles II welcomed a lean, contemplative French nobleman, ugly but amiable of countenance, and
ardent for philosophy: Charles Marguetel de Saint-Denis,
seigneur de Saint-Évremond. Unable to refrain from writing
and circulating a satire on Cardinal Mazarin, Saint-Évremond
had hastily removed himself from France in some dread of the
Bastille, a prison he knew well from an earlier occasion. Saint-
Évremond was a pupil of Pierre Gassendi, the French priest
who had reconstructed the text of Epicurus during the years
1647–9.[30] He described Gassendi as "the most knowing and
the least presuming of philosophers"; and in England, where he
remained until his death in 1704, Saint-Évremond became an
entrepreneur—slight, loquacious, but stimulating—between
fashionable society in London and the Epicurean followers of
Gassendi in Paris. "Monsieur St Évremond would talk for ever",
Pope told Joseph Spence.

Saint-Évremond soon made the acquaintance of Hobbes:
in his view, "the greatest genius of England since Bacon".[31]
He also won the friendship of Waller and corresponded with
Cowley's patron, the Earl of St. Albans. He collaborated with

the Duke of Buckingham in writing a comedy called *Sir Politick Would-Be*. Dryden esteemed him, and contributed an introductory note to the 1692 English translation of Saint-Évremond's letters. From 1675, when she in turn fled to England, Saint-Évremond frequented the salon of Charles II's favourite, Hortense, Duchesse de Mazarin, the reckless libidinous niece of the cardinal who had driven Saint-Évremond from France. He still visited her house at the time of her death twenty-five years later: Cyrano grown old, calling upon his ageing Roxana.

Saint-Évremond was soon appointed by an admiring Charles II, Keeper of the Ducks in St. James's Park.[32] Chelsea and St. James's were as far as the indolent Saint Évremond cared to stray from the environs of the Palais-Royal—in one of his letters he writes of his detestation of such distant places as China: "no wine in the whole empire, no olive oil, no butter, no oysters". In other letters he recommends St. Albans to follow the example of Epicurus by settling in the suburbs of the capital with a mistress and a handful of congenial friends; and compares Buckingham to Petronius "par mille endroits" but chiefly in the regularity of his irregular pleasures.[33]

His study of the morals of Epicurus was written in 1685 in the form of a long letter to the bluestocking, Ninon de Lenclos. The letter arose from the discourse concerning Epicurus by the poet Sarasin, another disciple of Gassendi. Saint-Évremond disagrees with Sarasin's interpretation of pleasure, in the Epicurean sense, as being austere and self-denying. The Epicurean who pursues Sarasin's *volupté sainte et sévère*, Saint-Évremond notes, practises a pleasure more rigorous that the virtue of the Stoics. "*Il goûte la volupté sans volupté*".[34] Sarasin had "talked of nothing but spiritual pleasures". Saint-Évremond asks what reason a philosopher who denied the immortality of the soul had to mortify the senses. Epicurus merely managed his pleasures with discretion:

But if he loved the enjoyment of them as a voluptuous person, he managed himself prudently; and as he was indulgent to the motions of Nature, so he disliked that any violence should be offered to it; not always reckoning chastity for a virtue, but always accounting luxury a vice.[35]

Saint-Évremond's existence, it must be confessed, was for the most part an idling and mannered one; but he was more than an urbane French wag, archly hobnobbing with earls and bluestockings, and docketting one trifle, glossing another. In the history of ideas he has a place as Gassendi's spokesman in Restoration England; and the charm of this keeper of the royal ducks and enthusiast of ancient learning was no shallow facility. When Pope called upon him at the end of his life, he found him at home surrounded by his pet animals and feeding the birds which ran about the house: "a great Epicure", said Pope, "and a great sloven":

> He had a great variety of these and other sorts of animals all over the house, and used always to say that "when we grow old, and our own spirits decay, it reanimates one to have a number of living creatures about one, and to be much with them".[36]

Creech's translation of Lucretius only sped on its way an Epicurean movement which had started among the dramatists some time before. Sir George Etherege, in one of those hours of penitence which now and then broke into the life of riot he customarily led, wrote to a friend: "I used to be a gadabout and love roving, but I have suddenly become a disciple of Epicurus. I stay in my little haven, and I have set up as my maxim that the greatest pleasure consists in perfect health. The ecstasy of a debauch fails to compensate for the depression one suffers the morning after."[37] No doubt Etherege's resolution lasted as long as his hangover; but whatever his life was, his comedies remain Epicurean.

The sentiments voiced by Nature, in Lucretius's lines on the folly of fearing death, pervade *She Would If She Could*. Etherege's theme is jaded appetite. A gloom of sexual ennui hangs over the play. The principles of *She Would If She Could* are those stated by Angelica in Congreve's *Love for Love*:

Uncertainty and Expectation are the Joys of Life. Security is an insipid thing, and the overtaking and possessing of a Wish, discovers the Folly of the Chase.[38]

Mr. Tattle, even during the course of seducing Miss Prue in *Love for Love*, envisages a boring conclusion to the experience.

For Etherege's bachelors, Mr. Freeman and Mr. Courtall, for Sir Oliver Cockwood, and even for the nymphomaniac Lady Cockwood, Nature runs the round again, the round it ran before. Just as in Etherege's *The Comical Revenge* the French valet's references to the pox repeatedly suggest, like a memento mori, the probable consequences of promiscuity; in *She Would If She Could* habit is represented as inimical to constant love. As Etherege sees it, most men have a promiscuous character: some suppress it, some never have the chance to show it, and some are lazy. Sir Oliver Cockwood is satiated by his wife and drained by his extra-marital intrigues. He must kiss and fawn and toy, he says, and lie fooling when, were it not for the disgrace's sake, he would rather "stand all that while in the pillory, pelted with rotten eggs and apples".[39] Lady Cockwood is described as "an old puss who has been coursed by most of the young fellows of her country".[40] Freeman and Courtall first take the stage regretting the lack of variety in the town. "Faith", laments Freeman, "I think we must e'en follow the old trade; eat well, and prepare ourselves with a bottle or two of good Burgundy, that our old acquaintance may look lovely in our eyes; for, for ought as I see, there is no hopes of new."[41] But across the wearied scene flit two fresh new things: Gatty and Ariana, newly come to town, glad to have escaped from the country, and affording to Freeman and Courtall at least a temporary alleviation.

Etherege's Dorimant is equalled only by Wycherley's Horner as a type of vicious or Petronian Epicurean. In *The Man of Mode* Dorimant discards his mistress, Loveit, and is encouraged as a suitor by the heiress, Harriet Woodvil. The lust for power, by which he may define others rather than be himself defined by them, tinctures all Dorimant's dealings with women. It is conspicuous in his dismissal of Loveit, after which he goes on to exercise the same gratifying dominance on Belinda, repelled though she is by his treatment of her predecessor. He despises women for the life of thoughtless sensation they lead—all except Harriet. He wants "to pluck off the mask and show the passion that's panting under".[42] Whilst seducing Belinda, Dorimant also woos Harriet and encourages his friend Bellair to marry Emilia so that Dorimant may come at her more easily.

Dorimant in his ceremonious depravity, his careful and well-measured viciousness, regards love as an intellectual game. A matador skirting and side-stepping the bull of desire, to the guileful contest he brings all his expertness. One suspects that his sexual drive is relatively slight. There appear to be four elements in his dedication to the chase: vainglory; the malicious indulgence of a sense of power over others; a taste for variety; and an Epicurean distaste for passion qualified by an Epicurean curiosity about its nature. The nature of love, and the potency of his own charm, provide Dorimant with many opportunities, not only to dominate the will of others, but to dispose of their fates from a mocking Olympian height. Predator, conforming to no tradition of behaviour, relying absolutely on his own unquestionable abilities, Dorimant, in his self-assertive aggression, partially conforms to the type of Natural Man described in Hobbes's *Leviathan*: pre-social Man of "the time, wherein men live without other security, than what their own strength, and their own invention shall furnish them withall" and "every man is Enemy to every man".[43] The elegance of Dorimant's manner does not detract from the belligerence of his purpose. In order to extend his own will he is an enemy to all men, and particularly to all women.

The third element in Dorimant's libertinism, his taste for variety, is the product of the satiated sexuality which casts a pall over *She Would If She Could*. Like Courtall and Freeman he dreads the boredom of a defined future. What stimulates Dorimant is the transferred hazard, the reopened gamble, the falter of the tongue, the catch of the breath and the bounce of the heart. From his putative original, the Earl of Rochester,

Dorimant has acquired (in addition to considerable classical learning and a love for repeating aloud scraps of poetry which have caught his fancy) an admiration for Lucretius and Epicurean philosophy. Lucretius recommended a detachment from all social and doctrinal concerns; in which detachment, like a dispassionate god, one should rationally and systematically investigate human experience. Dorimant's exploration of feeling is akin to that of the English Epicureans of the 1890s who, led by Walter Pater, believed that success in life inheres in the failure to form habits.

In the comedies of John Dryden it is hard to discern a philosophical partisanship; only a pure intelligence, bland, unzealous and at ease. In his most heartfelt dramatic work, the *Secular Masque*, the sentiment—the despair of modern times, the hope that a golden past will be renewed—is Stoical; and although Dryden trifled with Epicureanism, and translated Lucretius with vigour and discernment, he condemns the Epicurean philosophy in his preface to that translation; also in his *Religio Laici*, and in the most striking of the occasional passages in his plays which draw upon Lucretius's words. The passage occurs in *Tyrannic Love*, a tragedy about St. Catherine which he published in 1670. The Emperor Maximin's emissary, Placidus, woos St. Catherine on Maximin's behalf, offering her rank and wealth. St. Catherine replies with a paraphrase of the opening of the Second Book of *De Rerum Natura*; comparing "the unknown, untalked-of man" to a hermit who, from the security of his cell on the cliff, watches a vessel fraught with treasure wrecked by "mad tempests":

> And when from far the tenth wave does appear,
> Shrinks up in silent joy, that he's not there.[44]

Placidus, a scholar, recognises the allusion to Lucretius, and asks St. Catherine why, if she is an Epicurean, she wastes time in prayers; upon which she denies that she is an Epicurean, and produces an argument which, in her view, confutes "him, who thought A casual world was from wild atoms wrought": the rare workmanship of the Universe implies a workman. This argument was often used in the seventeenth and eighteenth centuries, not so much against Epicureanism as against the atheism with which Epicureanism had come to be associated.

It says a great deal for the learning, and even for the tolerance of the Restoration public, that Thomas Shadwell was able to start the first scene of his comedy *The Virtuoso*, of 1674, by making his hero quote, in the original Latin, Lucretius's lines about the indifference of the Gods. The quotation is followed by a dialogue between Bruce, the hero, and his friend Longvil:

> LONGVIL. *Bruce*, Good Morrow: What great author art thou chewing the Cud upon? I look'd to have found you with your Head-ake and your Morning-Qualms.
> BRUCE. We should not live always hot-headed; we should give ourselves leave sometimes to think.
> LONGVIL. *Lucretius*! Divine *Lucretius*! But my Noble Epicurean, what an Unfashionable Fellow art thou, that in this Age art given to understand *Latin*.[45]

Bruce and Longvil agree to follow a code of Epicurean rationality. To them this means, since Epicurus did not positively forbid self-indulgence, a code of dispassionate pleasure-seeking. But Shadwell, by an old dramatic contrivance, shows how easily they jettison their philosophy when under the involuntary stress of love and anger; so that these two would-be philosophers conclude by fighting each other like brutes. (Shadwell's comedies are Aristophanic in the sense that they are essentially conservative, and mock innovation. In the person of the Virtuoso himself Shadwell ridicules the other aspect of Epicureanism: the study of natural causes by experimental science.) Aphra Behn's heroes, Mr. Galliard in *The Feigned Courtesans* and Tom Wilding in *The City Heiress*, may also be regarded as defeated Epicureans, who in the end acquiesce in the commonplaces of impulsive humanity.

"As we have no affections, so we have no malice", says Sparkish in Wycherley's *Country Wife*. Both Horner and Sparkish practise a dispassionate sensuality; Sparkish, however, merely modishly and foolishly. Horner pretends that he has found an antidote against the pox, "and that worse distemper, love".[46] He prefers the uncomplicated appetite of lust—that noble reflux of vigorous blood, as Congreve's old Bachelor calls it. Horner sees in Mrs. Pinchwife no more than a silly mistress, soon got, soon lost: "a damned loving changeling".[47] But Mrs. Pinchwife herself, a creature who lives in a state of nature, has the distemper badly. In her soliloquy at the end of the Fourth Act of *The Country Wife*, she extends Horner's metaphor. She has, she says, "the London disease called love". She has heard "this distemper" called a fever, but she thinks it is more like an ague, since her husband makes her cold whilst Horner makes her hot: *then* she is "all in a fever indeed".[48] Horner has, as he claims, found a remedy for this distemper: in the emasculation, not (as he pretends) of his body, but of his passions. Throughout the play, Pinchwife, as the passionate man, is contrasted with Horner; and as a passionate man is represented as injurious to himself and others. "I wear a sword", he tells Horner. "It should be taken from thee", replies Horner, "lest thou shouldst do thyself a mischief with it."[49] There is, however, a strong and unphilosophical infusion of spite in the nature of Horner. Congreve's Mirabell, who benignly marries off his former mistress, is better disposed towards his partners in his life of cool, rational pleasure; and therefore the better Epicurean.

For his characters Wycherley entertains an urbane but weighty malevolence. Aphra Behn at least displays an amused affection for her clowns, such as Sir Signal Buffoon, and is swept off her feet by the heroes she modelled upon the fatal John Hoyle. With Wycherley there is nothing but disdain. He is loftily disengaged from the fates of his characters. There is a burly sarcastic strength in his contempt for the vapid young men whose misdeeds and maraudings he recounts, without liking, in *Love in a Wood*. Behind the Petronian "science of voluptuousness", in Wycherley's plays, lies no love of his fellow-men. Poor Mr. Paris, in *The Gentleman Dancing Master*, for all his good nature, is bitterly tricked and married off to a common woman of the town. Not even for the hero does that play end sunnily, since the heroine makes it plain that once she has married him she will feel at liberty to cuckold him if she pleases. Gerrard refers to "the sage maxim of your sex, which is, wittols make the best husbands, that is, cuckolds". His remark leads to a frank exchange with Hippolita:

HIPPOLITA. For, I say, you are to be my Husband, and you say Husbands must be Wittals, and some strange things to boot.
GERRARD. Well, I will take my Fortune.
HIPPOLITA. But have a care, rash man.
GERRARD. I will venture.
HIPPOLITA. At your peril remember I wish'd you to have a care, forewarn'd, fore-arm'd.[50]

All four of Wycherley's plays are cool statements of his colossal, though smiling, misanthropy.

Congreve's Mirabell in his patient ruthlessness, Farquhar's Sir Harry Wildair in his merry nonchalance, and Vanbrugh's Lord Foppington in his arch disdain, all conform in their different ways to the type of the Epicurean gentleman. Sir Harry's way is an airy, bouncing one. He never allows himself to abandon his good-humour, or to display displeasure. Even when he is obliged by his gentlemanly code to thrash a City merchant who has impugned his honour, he does so in the jolliest way, taking snuff, with many civil regrets: "Sir, I beg you ten thousand pardons, but I am absolutely condemned to't upon my honour, sir; nothing can be more averse to my inclinations." He takes pleasure in resenting an injury without passion, and says that this is the beauty of revenge.[51]

In his impassivity and sang-froid Sir Harry represents an ideal of male conduct which remained a national one until recent times. He enshrines the same virtues as such national heroes as Nelson and Wellington. His love, he says: 'is only a pitch of gratitude; while she loves me, I love her; when she desists, the obligation's void".[52] Learning that Lady Lurewell has betrayed him and his friend Colonel Standard simultaneously, he bursts not with spleen but with laughter:

O the delight of an ingenious Mistriss! What life and briskness it adds to an Amour, like the Loves of mighty *Jove*, still sueing in different shapes![53]

He comes wooing Angelica with the brisk words, "By all the dust of my ancient progenitors, I must this night quarter my coat-of-arms with yours!" Mistaking her house for a brothel, he offers her fifty guineas. Later discovering his appalling mistake, he "looks foolish and hums a song".[54]

Amongst the characters of Restoration Comedy, only Millamant is more memorable than Lord Foppington. They are both egoists on an Olympian scale, and utterly regardless of the opinions or estimation of the mortals among whom they have alighted. In his cool but undeviating arrogance Lord Foppington is a Coriolanus in ribbons. He follows the cult of himself. He cares for nobody's franchise. He also has the Epicurean faults of selfishness and coldness of heart, which Vanbrugh takes occasion to reprobate—although lightly. Lord Foppington is contrasted with his brother, Tom Fashion, a careless rake; yet the contrast is hardly that between Blifil and Tom Jones.

Punctiliously Lord Foppington carries out the obligations of the Epicurean dandy as they are described, for example, in the intimate journals of Charles Baudelaire.[55] He never talks to people except to baffle them. He is proud of not being so low as the people he passes in the street. He aspires to being sublime without interruption, and lives and sleeps in front of a looking-glass. Baudelaire continues to define the dandy in his study of Romantic painting: Dandyism is the pleasure of surprising and the proud satisfaction of never being surprised oneself. A dandy can be a heartless man or a man in pain; but in the latter case, he smiles like the Spartan youth gnawed by the fox under his cloak. Dandyism is the last flash of heroism in a decayed society. Dandyism is a setting sun: superb, without warmth, and melancholy.[56] Especially in the later scenes of *The Relapse*, Lord Foppington illustrates all these qualities of the dandy in the Baudelairean sense.

It is the reflection he sees in the looking-glass which matters to Lord Foppington, not the reflection in the eyes of others. He loves to see himself all round. He does not scan the glass in approbation but as a scrupulous exercise in self-criticism.

E

Without illusions, he knows himself: what endears him to the ladies, he remarks, is not his person but the peerage which he has just purchased:

> Why, the Ladies were ready to Pewke at me, whilst I had nothing but Sir *Novelty* to recommend me to 'em—Sure, whilst I was but a Knight, I was a very nauseous Fellow—Well, 'tis Ten Thousand Pawnd well given—stap my Vitals.[57]

Offended by Amanda's insolent virtue, and thinking himself piqued as a matter of honour to debauch her, Lord Foppington makes his way to Loveless's town house, where the reconciled couple have just arrived from the quiet, well-behaved country. Expansive, he favours Amanda with an account of his daily round; and in an excess of cynicism, thinking that his newly purchased peerage will blind her to all else, Lord Foppington plunges carelessly in at Amanda's virtue. He thus has to fight her naturally infuriated husband. "He's a very beastly fellow," Lord Foppington later remarks, "in my opinion."

Although he likes to unbend his mind with such pranks as his flirtation with Amanda, Lord Foppington has a great deal of common sense. As Amanda points out, he is no fool. He does not merely practise the Petronian, or pseudo-Epicurean science of voluptuousness. He is not what Sir Thomas Browne calls a "novice in true Epicureanism, which by mediocrity, paucity, quick and healthful Appetite, makes delights smartly acceptable".[58] He has the genuine Epicurean characteristics of self-containment, self-definition and scepticism. Admittedly, he is not fond of the inside of books: "For to mind the inside of a Book is to entertain oneself with the forc'd Product of another Man's Brain. Naw I think a Man of Quality and Breeding may be much diverted with the Natural Sprauts of his own."[59]

When his imprudent younger brother, Tom Fashion, having squandered his own fortune, rhetorically appeals to Lord Foppington's sentiments, threatening that unless he is given £500 he will turn highwayman, Lord Foppington replies:

> Why, Faith, *Tam*—to give you my Sense of the Thing, I do think taking a Purse the best Remedy in the World; for if you succeed,

you are reliev'd that way; if you are taken—you are reliev'd t'other.[60]

He does not wish Tom Fashion to suppose that he can be played upon. In his bearing towards his brother at least, Lord Foppington justifies his description of himself:

Why, my Heart in my Amours—is like my Heart aut of my Amours: à la glace. My Bady, *Tam*, is a Watch; and my Heart is the Pendulum to it; whilst the Finger runs raund to every Hour in the Circle, that still beats the same time.[61]

Lord Foppington has contracted to marry fifteen hundred pounds a year and, attached to it, the primitive lewd daughter of Sir Tunbelly Clumsey, a country magistrate. The parties to the marriage have not yet met. In revenge, Tom Fashion goes down to Sir Tunbelly's house, impersonates Lord Foppington, and secretly marries Hoyden, the daughter, himself. When Lord Foppington arrives, it is he who is taken for the impostor. He is kept waiting at the gate:

A Pax of these bumpkinly People, will they open the Gate, or do they desire I should grow at their Moat-side like a Willow? Hey, Fellow—Prithee do me the Favour, in as few words as thou canst find to express thyself, to tell me whether thy Master will admit me or not, that I may turn about my Coach, and be gone.[62]

Hardly has Lord Foppington been admitted than he is seized, disarmed and tied up. With disdainful calm he surveys the new situation:

Naw do I begin to believe I am a-Bed and asleep, and that all this is but a dream—If it be, 'twill be an agreeable surprise enough, to waken by an by; and instead of the impertinent Company of a Nasty Country Justice, find myself perhaps, in the arms of a Woman of Quality.[63]

Eventually released, he finds that Hoyden has already married Tom Fashion. Perhaps he feels some relief, having now met Hoyden. Hoyden is prepared to be married to either or both of them, so long as she can escape her father and run loose in London, but of the two she prefers Tom Fashion, since Lord Foppington reminds her of an old horse she once had called Washy. Drily Lord Foppington congratulates his brother:

> LORD FOPPINGTON. (*Aside.*) Naw for my part I think the wisest thing a Man can do with an aking heart, is to put on a serene Countenance, for a Philosaphical Air is the most becoming thing in the World to the face of a Person of Quality; I will therefore bear my Disgrace like a Great Man, and let the People see I am above an affrant. (*To Young Fashion.*) Dear *Tam*, since Things are thus fallen aut, prithee give me leave to wish thee Jay. I do it *de bon Cœur*, strike me dumb: you have marry'd a Woman Beautiful in her Person, Charming in her Ayrs, Prudent in her Canduct, Canstant in her Inclinations, and of a Nice Marality, split my windpipe.
>
> YOUNG FASHION. Your lordship may keep up your Spirits with your Grimace if you please, I shall support mine with this Lady and two Thousand Pound a year.[64]

Tom has taken his purse and achieved a happiness which depends less on his will than on the two thousand pounds a year. Lord Foppington is the poorer for not marrying Hoyden: he must retrench in the articles of periwigs and the powder for them. But his spirits do not depend on supports outside himself. Even if he lost his whole fortune, he would still retain his serene countenance and his philosophical air: "not pleased by good deeds, nor provoked by bad".

It is well-known that Vanbrugh's "Sir Novelty Fashion, newly created Lord Foppington" was borrowed from Cibber's *Love's Last Shift*. Cibber's Sir Novelty, however, differs in many ways from Vanbrugh's utterly self-sufficient dandy, who courts only his own not easily won approval. Cibber's Sir Novelty "affects mightily to ridicule himself, only to give others a kind of necessity of praising him".[65] He solicits others for their votes in his favour: "For heaven's sake deal freely with me, madam, and tell me, if you can, one tolerable thing about me."[66] He is undignified. He lacks the grim ironical phlegm that Vanbrugh's Lord Foppington always musters at moments of vexation. He is capable of outright incivility: "Demn your house, your family, your ancestors, your generation and your eternal posterity."[67] A self-advertiser, he is going to write a play "in vindication of all well-dressed gentlemen".[68]

The Relapse was not the end of Lord Foppington. Vanbrugh passed him back to Cibber, who used him in *The Careless Husband* of 1704. There has been some coarsening of the tissues, and Cibber makes Lord Foppington a little too noisy, but he remains an amusingly self-willed personage, and he has added some new oaths, including "Sunburn me!", to his range. One is glad to have more of him. Lord Foppington has married, in order to separate himself as much as possible from his wife; for he thinks that "deferring a dun, and getting rid of one's wife, are two of the most agreeable sweets in the liberty of an English subject".[69] Whilst he sends his wife off to London, a town which he deems to have fallen into the hands of the wrong people, he retires to the bucolic peace of Windsor. Capriciously, and for the most part unsuccessfully, he sets up as an amorist. The bustle of his attempts on various young women's virtue captivates his mind more than the effect of them. They produce in him sensations which, although intriguing to him as matter to ponder upon, disturb neither his understanding nor his self-will. When Lady Betty Modish declines to commit adultery with him, he tells himself :

> I am struck dumb by the Deliberation of her Assurance; and do not positively remember, that the *Non-Chalence* of my Temper ever had so bright an Occasion to show itself before.[70]

Then, with a secret curse or two at her impertinence, this curious being wings on his way, contriving brief confusions, in his coach-and-six: "I Love to have creatures go as I bid them. . . . Foppington's long-tails are known in every road in England."[71] His emotions also go as he bids them.

In 1777 Sheridan wrote a cleaned-up version of *The Relapse*, which he reduced from twenty to twelve scenes and called *A Trip to Scarborough*. Every change which Sheridan made, except for his shortening of the sentimental scenes, was for the worse.

Sheridan cuts out many of the oaths and all references to Lord Foppington's guts. The consciences of Loveless and Berinthia are stricken by their overhearing Amanda express her trust in them, and they reform at once. Sir Tunbelly does not refer to Hoyden's changing her linen. The sex of Old Coupler the marriage-broker is changed from male to female, which is as well, in view of his overtures to Tom Fashion. Sheridan whittles away many of Lord Foppington's most sublimely frivolous utterances, and paraphrases others—an impudence which Lord Foppington would have much resented. And indeed, a word taken away from the part of Lord Foppington in *The Relapse* could not be other than the spoiling of one kind of perfection, however small the scale of that perfection. It would be a note left out of a sonata by Scarlatti, a chip off the nose of a figure in Chelsea china, a lacuna in Epicurus's own holograph.

CHAPTER SIX

Bright Nymphs of Britain

HARRIET WOODVIL, in *The Man of Mode*, marks the first stage in an important transition in Restoration Comedy: from the lover as the centre of interest to his lady as the centre of interest. Millamant in *The Way of the World* comes to play the part assigned to Dorimant in *The Man of Mode*. The heroine, not the hero, subjugates all, and indulges every caprice. There were several reasons, literary, theatrical, and social, for the transition; amongst them the expert feminist propaganda of Mrs. Behn, the rise of such accomplished actresses as Mrs. Bracegirdle and Mrs. Barry, the increasing patronage of the playhouses by respectable women, and the evidences of feminine power provided by the royal mistresses. Aphra Behn dedicated a play to Nell Gwynne, and the career of the Duke of Marlborough was founded on his ability to please the Duchess of Cleveland. In her witty and self-standing pertness Harriet anticipates Millamant. In her capacity, her self-assurance and her unwillingness to defer to men without good reason, she is the predecessor of the heroines of the Hanoverian novel: Richardson's haughty and independent Clarissa, Smollett's dauntless Emilia Gauntlett, Fielding's all-providing, quietly all-managing Amelia Booth. The New Woman was new long before the time of H. G. Wells and Bernard Shaw. The heroines of Etherege's plays were the pioneers of that war-band so intimidating to the male sex.

It was appropriate that Nell Gwynne was the actress chosen to recite the suffragette epilogue to Aphra Behn's *Sir Patient Fancy* at its first production. The epilogue opens with an objection to the prejudice of men, even the most witless and insignificant ones, against women writers:

> I here and there o'erheard a Coxcomb cry,
> Ah, Rot it—'tis a Woman's Comedy . . .
> What has poor Woman done, that she must be
> Debar'd from Sense, and sacred Poetry?

In the past women have shown themselves capable of famous deeds and writings. They have governed well, and fought successfully in battle:

> We still have passive Valour, and can show,
> Wou'd Custom give us leave, the active too,
> Since we no Provocations want from you.
> For who but we cou'd your dull Fopperies bear,
> Your saucy Love, and your brisk Nonsense hear?

Aphra Behn is ready to defer to men who can justify their claim to better sense, but not to coxcombs with their "worse than womanish Affectation":

> To all the Men of Wit we will subscribe:
> But for your half Wits, ye unthinking Tribe,
> We'll let you see, whate'er besides we do,
> How artfully we copy some of you:
> And if you're drawn to th' Life, pray tell me then,
> Why women should not write as well as men.[1]

Aphra Behn's competitive feelings are also embodied in the figure of the dominant woman which is common in her plays, although dominant in male terms. Perhaps, like Colette, she preferred effeminate men because they gave more sway to her own would-be masculinity. At the beginning of her play, *The Feigned Courtesans*, Laura, a young Italian aristocrat, leaves church for the love-nest she has rented and furnished in order to lure into it the not reluctant Mr. Galliard. It is a curious and Behn-like shift in the roles of the sexes. Laura says, "I would have this new habitation which I have designed for love known to none but him to whom I've destined my heart." She describes Mr. Galliard as "that dear Englese I must enjoy".[2] Often Aphra Behn's heroines dress up as men. In *The Feigned Courtesans* all the female characters occasionally disguise themselves as young men. It is interesting that two of them, when so disguised, attempt to fight duels with their lovers, using that aggressive male attribute, the sword. The two feigned courtesans, in flight from their families, disguise themselves as prostitutes, since prostitution is the only calling in which they can avoid men's impertinent concern for their welfare, exercise their wits independently, and come and go as they please. Improbably, they preserve their honour in this role.

Gatty and Ariana, in Etherege's *She Would If She Could*, are the first pair of those female comrades-in-arms who often appear in Restoration Comedy, practical she-Epicureans both. They are assertive young women—girl-gallants—who envy men their freedom, and so gad about in the masks which had recently become fashionable. "Well", says Gatty, "we cannot plague 'em enough when we have it in our power for those privileges which custom has allowed 'em above us":

> ARIANA. The truth is, they can run and ramble here, and there, and every where, and we poor Fools rather think the better of 'em.
> GATTY. From one Play-house, to the other Play-house, and if they like neither the Play nor the Women, they seldom stay any longer than the combing of their Perriwigs, or a whisper or two with a Friend; and then they cock their Caps, and out they strut again.
> ARIANA. But whatsoever we do, prithee let us resolve to be mighty honest.
> GATTY. There I agree with thee.[3]

And "mighty honest" they are, in spite of their bravado—in spite of Gatty's male view of marriage: "Without the allowance of vanity, an amour would grow as dull as matrimony." But her emancipated notions do not prevent her from marrying Mr. Courtall.

We first catch sight of Etherege's later heroine, Harriet Woodvil, as she refuses to stand still for her maid to tidy her hair:

> BUSY. Dear Madam! Let me set that Curl in order.
> HARRIET. Let me alone, I will shake 'em all out of order.

BUSY. Will you never leave this Wildness?
HARRIET. Torment me not. . . . How do I daily suffer from thy Officious Fingers.[4]

Tranquillity and order are conditions that Harriet detests. In her small outrages and desperate bouts of energy and dogmatism she plunges about like an intemperate salmon, all flounce and disappearing tail. She is the earliest of the Suffragettes. She utterly disagrees with Luther's impudent saying that God gave women plump hindquarters so that they should sit at home on them. Sit at home! Harriet is unwilling to stand on two feet if one will do. At the end of *The Man of Mode* she is indignant at having to return to the country, and does not exactly encourage Dorimant to visit her among her rooks; but she is willing to tolerate male silliness if he should do so:

DORIMANT. The first time I saw you, you left me with the pangs of Love upon me, and this day my soul has quite given up her liberty.
HARRIET. This is more dismal than the Country, Emilia! Pity me, who am going to that sad place.[5]

Harriet's speech is not far from Millamant's "Well, you ridiculous thing you, I'll have you", on her acceptance of Mirabell. When Harriet tells Mrs. Loveit that Dorimant has been Loveit's God Almighty long enough, Harriet is expressing contempt more for Loveit's slavishness than for her poor morals.

Carolina and Lucia, in Shadwell's *Epsom Wells*, are copies of Gatty and Ariana in *She Would If She Could*, on which part of the plot of *Epsom Wells* is based. The scene in which, wandering alone in masks, they are molested by the hooligans Cuff and Kick is, however, Shadwell's own warning to young beauties of the perils they must face if they insist on a male freedom. Once again, in Shadwell's *The Virtuoso*, there are two female comrades in mischief, this time Clarinda and Miranda, nieces of the Virtuoso. Their behaviour to their great-uncle, the masochistic Mr. Snarl, is remarkably tomboyish. To tease him, they throw away his pipe and his cane, his hat and his periwig, and push him on the ground:

> SNARL. 'Ounds! you young Jades, I'll maul you, you Strumpets, you damn'd Cockatrices. I'll disinherit my Nephew, if he does not turn you out of Doors, you crocodills.
> CLARINDA. That's it we'd have, we'll weary both of your lives till you bring it about.[6]

Shadwell's third pair of female revolutionaries, pertly disordering a man-made world, are Isabella and Teresia in *The Squire of Alsatia*:

> ISABELLA. Well, it is a most painful life to dissemble constantly.
> TERESIA. 'Tis well we are often alone to unbend to one another, one had as good be a Player; and act continually, else.[7]

The quaint solidarity of these sisterly pairs in Restoration Comedy is always amusing.

Alone as a vivid character among the jigging marionettes of Shadwell's *Bury Fair* is Gertrude, a girl of independent mind and semi-masculine outlook, impatient with the situation of women in Restoration life. She is a Betjeman-ish girl, a Joan Hunter-Dunne, the kind of girl who would nowadays spend her time playing unreflecting tennis ("whizzing them over the nets, full of the strength of five") and her evenings smelling of face-cream, wool and the home counties; a great lover of horses. There are not many of them left now. With no helpfulness at all she suffers the courtship of Lord Bellamy: "How I hate this kind of fooling! A Woman never makes so silly a Figure, as when she is to look demurely, and stand to be made Love to."[8] A free-spoken girl, she shares her male contemporaries' apprehensions of marriage: "This same whoreson marriage kills all love and makes best friends fall out."

The philosophy of the girl-gallant is enunciated by Hippolita in Wycherley's *The Gentleman Dancing Master*. Hippolita is a girl of fourteen, confined to the house by her father. "O unnatural father", she says, "to shut up a poor girl at fourteen and hinder her budding." Her father has decided to marry

Hippolita to Mr. Paris, a good-natured clown of rich but low family; but, by Hippolita's own contrivance, Mr. Gerrard, the hero of the play, poses as a dancing master in order to carry her off. Having found means to bring Gerrard into her room at night, she tells herself to take courage:

> Courage then, *Hippolita*, make use of the only opportunity thou canst have to enfranchize thyself. Women formerly (they say) never knew how to make use of their time till it was past, but let it not be said so of a young Woman of this Age; my damn'd Aunt will be stirring presently: well then, courage, I say; *Hippolita*, thou art full fourteen years old, shift for thyself.[9]

Gerrard's fine speeches make her impatient: "Well, all this fooling but loses time, I must make better use of it." Provocatively, to put the idea into his head, she tells Gerrard that she is afraid he will abduct her:

> HIPPOLITA. Nay, I am sure you would carry me away, what should you come in at the Window for, if you did not mean to steal me?
> GERRARD. If I should endeavour it, you might cry out, and I should be prevented.
> HIPPOLITA. (*Aside*) Dull, dull man of the Town! are all like thee? He is as dull as a Country Squire at Questions and Commands. No, if I should cry out never so loud, this is quite at the further end of the House, and there nobody could hear me.[10]

Doubting Gerrard's sincerity, Hippolita pretends that she has no fortune of her own; to which he replies that without a fortune she will be so much the lighter and easier to carry away. Hippolita undeceives him at the end of the play: "I have the twelve hundred pounds a-year out of my father's power, which is yours, and I am sorry it is not the Indies to mend your bargain." She reminds him that she makes her fortune over to him not from want of dexterity and enterprise in managing it herself, but as a token of her love: "But sure, though I give myself and fortune away frankly, without the consent of my friends, my confidence is less than theirs who stand off only for separate maintenance."[11]

Congreve's Angelica, in teasing her uncle, talks bluff male bawdry, and in matters of business outdoes all the men in *Love for Love*. Not content with merely safeguarding her own fortune, she exercises her wits—none too honestly—to retrieve that of her lover, Valentine Legend.

Vanbrugh's equally systematic Berinthia, in *The Relapse*, is delighted when she can "with the expense of a few coquette glances, lead twenty fools about in a string".[12] She loves contrivance for its own sake:

> Besides, Faith, I begin to fancy there may be as much pleasure in carrying on another Bodies Intrigue, as one's own. This at least is certain, it exercises all the entertaining Faculties of a Woman.[13]

It is the "speculative", not "the practick part of all unlawful love", which pleases her best:

> AMANDA. The Practick Part of all unlawful love is—
> BERINTHIA. O 'tis abominable: But for the Speculative; that we must all confess is entertaining. The Conversation of all the Virtuous Women in the Town turns upon that and new cloaths.[14]

Berinthia, like Olivia in Wycherley's *The Plain Dealer*, submits to men in spite of an overt wish for independence, and a manifest ability to fend for herself. She would have agreed with Colette's dictum that free women are not women at all.

Vanbrugh renews, in *The Provoked Wife*, the device of the she-comrades so much favoured by Shadwell and Aphra Behn. Lady Brute and her cousin Belinda are fellow-conspirators against masculine authority ("confederating strumpets", Sir John Brute calls them). They reproach him for smoking his pipe: "Lord, Sir John, I wonder you won't leave that nasty custom." They sew and prattle after dinner when he desires to be left in peace to digest his own thoughts:

> BELINDA. We'll send for our Work and sit here.
> LADY BRUTE. He'll choak us with his Tobacco.
> BELINDA. Nothing will choak us, when we are doing what we have a mind to.[15]

Having liberated the house from Sir John, they exchange the delicious confidences he holds in such scorn:

> LADY BRUTE. Why I'll swear, *Bellinda*, some People do give strange agreeable Airs to their Faces in speaking. Tell me true!— Did you never practise in the Glass?
> BELINDA. Why, did you?
> LADY BRUTE. Yes, Faith, many a time.
> BELINDA. And I too, I own it; both how to speak myself, and how to look when others speak.

They discuss what sort of expression to assume when there is a bawdy joke in a play they are watching: "laugh we must not, though our stays burst for it":

> BELINDA. For my part I always take that Occasion to blow my Nose.
> LADY BRUTE. You must blow your Nose half off then at some Plays.[16]

Farquhar's *The Recruiting Officer* is a play chiefly animated by its tomboy heroine, Silvia. Withheld from the exuberant Captain Plume, upon whom she has set her heart, by her father, a Shrewsbury magistrate, she slips loose disguised as a young man, and enlists in Plume's regiment. She tries out first what it is like to be a soldier. She says that she wants to qualify herself, by her impudence, for the service. Her breeches, in her opinion, suit her as well as "any ranting fellow". The principal ingredients in the composition of a captain, she thinks, are a bold step, a rakish toss of the head, a smart cock of the hat and an impudent air:

> What's here: Rose! my nurse's daughter!—I'll go and practise.— Come, child, kiss me at once.—(*Kisses Rose*).

Her first military action is to save Rose's virtue from her new captain by claiming Rose as her own mistress; although Rose is not content with her cool bedfellow:

> SILVIA. What's the matter? did you not like your Bedfellow?
> ROSE. I don't know whether I had a Bedfellow or not.

SILVIA. Did not I lye with you?

ROSE. No—I wonder you could have the Conscience to ruine a poor Girl for nothing.

SILVIA. I have saved thee from Ruin, Child; don't be melancholy, I can give you as many fine things as the Captain can.

ROSE. But you can't, I'm sure.[17]

By a twist in the plot, Silvia is arrested for seducing Rose, and brought before her own father, who has her remanded in custody:

MR. BALANCE. Take this Gentleman into Custody till farther Orders.

ROSE. Pray your Worship, don't be uncivil to him, for he did me no Hurt. He's the most harmless Man in the World, for all he talks so.[18]

The play ends predictably, with Silvia marrying Captain Plume, and taking Rose into her service as a maid. Captain Plume sells his recruits, resigns his commission, and settles down in Shropshire to enjoy Silvia's fortune. The play rattles along, not very daintily, with an immense and engaging good humour, so that one is constantly reminded of Henry Fielding, with whom Farquhar had much in common.

Farquhar's Shrewsbury heroine, especially in the scene in which she quarrels with Melinda, is certainly not a gentle-woman in any sense that Congreve would have used. Indeed, Millamant does not quarrel, or become heated at all, except on one occasion when, irritated with Petulant and Witwoud, she slightly disorders her hair by tossing her head. A she-Epicurean who engages in pleasures rationally, and enjoys them delicately, Millamant is as self-contained as Lord Foppington himself. She reproduces the bored aggression of Dorimant in her song, *Love's but the Frailty of the Mind*, but only as a sham to tease Mrs. Marwood. She really seeks the free play of her imagination and individuality within marriage, not outside it. Heroines such as Millamant and Harriet Woodvil do not put themselves at a disadvantage. They silently observe the old cavalier decorums—partly out of shrewdness, but more because of their sense of their own value. Marriage with independence, as Millamant's comical Provisoes suggest, is their aim. "I'll never marry, unless I am first made sure of my Will and Pleasure," says Millamant as she agrees to marry Mirabell.[19] In fact, Mirabell's own independence is more in danger. Mirabell, like the old cavalier poet Cowley, dedicates himself to the aggrandisement of his mistress. He can say with Cowley himself:

> Study or action others may embrace;
> My love's my business, and my books her face.

It is no wonder that the heroine of Congreve's *The Old Bachelor* remarks that she has a great passion for Cowley:

> Ah so Fine! So extreamly fine! So everything in the World that I like.[20]

The contrast with Dorimant's treatment of Mrs. Loveit is strong; and is a contrast achieved partly by Millamant's purity and Loveit's impurity. "Let us be mighty honest," say Lady Cockwood's nieces, Gatty and Ariana, in *She Would If She Could*. Lady Cockwood, who has not been "mighty honest", is shown no sympathy in the play. According to her maid, she has had assignations in the private rooms of most of the eating houses in the town. When Mr. Courtall deserts her, Lady Cockwood moves on with shameless alacrity to his friend Mr. Freeman. She uses her maid as a go-between and brazenly lets her take any blame which is incurred. In spite of its reputed libertinage, there is a general contempt for promiscuous women in Restoration Comedy. The chaste are usually respected. "Take example from my misfortunes, Bellinda; if thou would'st be happy, give thy self wholly up to goodness," says Loveit at the end of the *The Man of Mode*.[21] That is poor Loveit's remedy for love.

The distaste for loose women, comically expressed, in Restoration Comedy is probably why it was found acceptable for Dorimant to discard Loveit so harshly (and Loveit's behaviour towards Sir Fopling Flutter is no kinder than Dorimant's behaviour towards her). If chastity is a thing of so little value, Lady Brute asks Mr. Constant in Vanbrugh's *The Provoked Wife*, "Why do you earnestly recommend it to your wives and daughters?" Constant's reply defeats his own purpose:

> CONSTANT. We recommend it to our Wives, Madam, because we would keep 'em to ourselves. And to our Daughters, because we would dispose of 'em to others.
> LADY BRUTE. 'Tis, then, of some Importance, it seems, since you can't dispose of 'em without it.[22]

Dorimant's cruel rationality is pitted against the passionate self-abandon of Loveit; Abraham discards Hagar. Dorimant actually relishes the situation which is normally one of the most obnoxious a man can face: his severing of his connection with a former mistress. One of Etherege's poems suggests that, in his own person, he was more humane than Dorimant in unwinding himself from the arms of his Calypso:

> Alas! no less than you I grieve
> My dying flame has no reprieve;
> For I can never hope to find,
> Should all the nymphs I court be kind,
>
> One beauty able to renew
> Those pleasures I enjoyed in you,
> When Love and Youth did both conspire
> To fill our breasts and veins with fire.[23]

But with Dorimant all feeling for Loveit has been superseded by his whim of setting Sir Fopling on her, in order to divert and impress the public with his own wit and powers of invention. Present at Loveit's final humiliation is Harriet, who adds to it the ageless scorn of a virtuous woman for her morally slovenly sisters: "Mr. Dorimant has been your God Almighty long enough, 'tis time to think of another."[24]

Although Mrs. Pinchwife shows herself to be better than the dissolute London ladies only in respect of her warmer heart, these London ladies are the target for Wycherley's satire in *The Country Wife*. In *The Gentleman Dancing Master* Wycherley has described a lady of fashion who sold herself to a waiter for 17s. 6d. in coach fares. Lady Fidget and her friends in *The Country Wife* are discreet but hearty Messalinas, incessantly betraying their husbands—as rapacious in their pursuit of men as of the blue china which has recently become fashionable. Because of his pretended deficiency, Mr. Horner can come and go like a household pet, observing and spying, but unlike a household pet able to report on what he sees: an Asmodeus. Having acquired her tame, legitimate man, Lady Fidget well-nigh devours him. At first the ladies are repelled by the notion of Horner's imperfection:

> HORNER. Nay, Madam, I beseech you stay, if it be but to see, I can be as civil to Ladies yet, as they would desire.
> LADY FIDGET. No, no, foh, you cannot be civil to Ladies.
> MRS. DAINTY FIDGET. You as civil as Ladies would desire?
> LADY FIDGET. No, no, no. (*Exeunt*)[25]

But when they find out the truth, they hound Horner even into his lodgings, where the famous scene of the china ensues, which gave so much scandal when the play was first produced.

In *The Country Wife* Wycherley insists that dramatists should draw exact portraits, including the pimples and the small-pox marks. "They must follow their copy, the age," says Dorilant.[26] The fine ladies in the audience were far from pleased by Wycherley's portraits of them. They outlawed *The Country Wife*, just as three years later they outlawed Aphra Behn's *Sir Patient Fancy*, another satire on the conduct of the wives of London. Wycherley's stubborn reply was only to return even more vigorously to his onslaught on the ladies in his next play, *The Plain Dealer*. Wycherley claims, in the dedication of *The Plain Dealer*, that it was only because he snatched off the ladies' masks that he offended them; and it may be true that women sometimes use prudishness to arm an antagonism existing for other reasons. Into *The Plain Dealer* Wycherley brings a discussion of *The Country Wife*. He puts the condemnation of it into the mouth of Olivia, his final and most maliciously finished representation of a London lady. In her indignation at the china-scene in *The Country Wife*, Olivia has broken all her own china:

> 'Tis now as unfit an ornament for a Ladies Chamber, as the Pictures that come from *Italy*, and other hot Countries, as appears by their nudities, which I alwayes cover, or scratch out, wheresoe'er I find 'em.[27]

Olivia cheats Manly out of his fortune, entrusted to her, runs mad for Fidelia disguised as a boy, swigs brandy in her closet and spits on the floor when she hears men spoken of. "O, believe me," she says, "'tis a filthy Play, and you may take my word for a filthy Play as soon as another's."[28]

In the debate which is ever-renewed in Restoration Comedy between constant and inconstant love, the heroines are generally the champions of faithfulness. "Bright nymphs of Britain", sing Dryden's alliterative shepherd-boys in *King Arthur*:

> Bright Nymphs of *Britain*, with Graces attended,
> Let not your Days without Pleasure expire;
> Honour's but empty, and when Youth is ended
> All Men will praise you, but none will desire.
> Let not Youth fly away without Contenting;
> Age will come soon enough for your Repenting.[29]

To this the shepherdesses reply that what is being proposed is a dangerous game for shepherdesses:

> Shepherd, Shepherd, leave Decoying,
> Pipes are sweet, a Summer's day;
> But a little after Toying,
> Women have the Shot to Pay.
>
> Here are Marriage-Vows for signing,
> Set their Marks that cannot write:
> After that, without Repining
> Play and Welcome, Day and Night.[30]

Here the shepherdesses give the shepherds marriage-contracts, after which everyone sings:

> Come, Shepherds, lead up, a lively Measure;
> The Cares of Wedlock, are Cares of Pleasure:
> And whether Marriage bring Joy, or Sorrow,
> Make sure of this Day, and hang to Morrow.[31]

Then they all dance two horn-pipes. The principles of the heroines of Restoration Comedy are higher ones, but they bear in mind the same considerations as Dryden's shepherdesses.

The most sustained contribution to the debate between constant and inconstant love is in Aphra Behn's *The Feigned Courtesans*. Constant love is represented by Marcella and the serious and courtly Sir Harry Fillamour; inconstant love is represented by Cornelia and the flippant Mr. Galliard. It is the contention of the Flower and the Leaf again, but in a decorous perspective of Palladian architecture. Fillamour and Galliard take up an easy although graceful stance and, with a ceremonious familiarity, exchange their opinions like snuff-boxes. Although he has been in Rome for no more than a month, Mr. Galliard has already debauched a dozen Roman ladies. Sir Harry Fillamour, on the other hand, declares that to him there is no pleasure like constancy:

> GALLIARD. Constancy! and wou'dst thou have me one of those dull Lovers, who believe it their Duty to love a Woman till her Hair and Eyes change Colour, for fear of the scandalous Name of an Inconstant? No, my Passion, like great Victors, hates the lazy stay; but having vanquisht, prepares for new Conquests.
> FILLAMOUR. Which you gain as they do Towns by Fire, lose 'em even in the taking.[32]

For love of Fillamour, Marcella has run away from the marriage which her family has tried to force on her. With her she brings Cornelia, her wilful little sister just loose from a convent school. They disguise themselves as Roman courtesans, since this enables them to wear masks and escape the detection of their family. Cornelia wanders in the gardens of the Villa Medici joyously reading Ovid's *Art of Love* and exclaiming, with a Restoration dislike of the open air, "And prithee what a

pox have we to do with flowers, fountains or naked statues?"
And what are Marcella and Cornelia talking about in the
gardens of the Villa Medici? They too, by one of Mrs. Behn's
coincidences, are debating constant and inconstant love.

Cornelia delights in shocking her older and steadier sister,
and takes the side of inconstant love. "There's no merchandise
like ours, like that of love, my sister."[33] Marcella in reply rebukes
her: "A too forward maid, Cornelia, hurts her own fame and
that of her sex." The remark comes from the mouth of a girl
who, in pursuit of her lover, has come to Rome disguised as a
prostitute. The whole situation is paradoxical. Here are two
decent and respectable girls, of patrician family, out at night
in the Medici gardens, pretending to be prostitutes, deferring
all would-be customers, and discoursing of the nature of love.
Aphra Behn has that awareness of the face and the mask which
also pervades the plays of Wycherley. Cornelia asks Marcella if
she is afraid of the mask which she has voluntarily put on: that
of vice. Perhaps Aphra Behn saw herself and other women as
not so much given to vice as willing to use it as a counter in
their dealings with the world. As one of the characters in the
play says, whores "generally own their trade of sin, which
others deal by stealth in".

Thinking that Marcella is the famous Roman courtesan
Silvanietta, Mr. Galliard brings Sir Harry Fillamour to visit
her. He is anxious to corrupt Sir Harry, whose virtue irritates
him: "In that one sinner", says Mr. Galliard, "there are
charms that would excuse even to thee all frailty. . . . A rapture
now, dear lad, and then fall to."[34] Behind her mask Marcella
remains unknown to Sir Harry, but she recognises him, of
course, and is thus obliged to act the outward forms of a
prostitute to the man she loves. At least the situation gives
Marcella an opportunity, unusual in those days for one of her
class, to witness the unrestrained behaviour of her suitor. Sir
Harry, in fact, does well in the test. Becoming sentimental over
the beauty of the supposed courtesan, he tries to reclaim her
from her depraved life. Marcella is compelled by her disguise
to defend the trade of courtesan. One cannot forbear to admire

the wit with which Aphra Behn's characters sustain their shifts of identity. In the present instance, the man wants to safeguard the modesty which the woman pretends to be anxious to sacrifice to him, although she has no intention of really doing so.

So the debate on constant and inconstant love opens again. Mr. Galliard breaks in from time to time with his fervent support for anything Marcella says in favour of unchastity. The argument on each side is also followed with great interest by Sir Signal Buffon, who is hiding up the chimney. Sir Signal puts in an aside here and there: "peeping out of the chimney, his face blacked", say Mrs. Behn's stage directions, then "peeping out with a face more smutted", and finally "peeping more black". Sir Signal Buffoon, a harmless and indeed engaging fop, is on the Grand Tour with his tutor, Dr. Tickletext. Sir Signal wants hard to be wicked but can never quite manage it. As soon as they arrive in Rome, Sir Signal and Dr. Tickletext, unknown to each other, set out for the same Roman bawdy house, or what they take to be a bawdy house. With great humour Sir Signal learns that it is near the Hospital for Incurables: "very well situated", he observes, "in case of disaster". By mistake Dr. Tickletext and Sir Signal go to Marcella's lodging, where Sir Signal takes cover during the conversation between Marcella and Sir Harry Fillamour. Here ensues one of those scenes of farcical invention which Mrs. Behn loved to write. Dr. Tickletext, prowling in the garden, falls down the well. "Stumbles at the well", the stage directions state, "gets hold of the rope and slides down in the bucket." Sir Signal, when he emerges from his chimney, comes out to the well to wash off the soot. He hauls up the bucket, cursing at its weight, and is surprised to be confronted by Dr. Tickletext, the guardian of his morals.

Marcella's pose prevents her from assenting when Sir Harry demonstrates the rightness of her own point of view. He urges her to be constant to one man. She replies:

> Unconscionable! constant at my years?
> —Oh 'twere to cheat a thousand,

Who between this and my dull Age of Constancy,
Expect the distribution of my Beauty.[35]

Sir Harry begs her to make one man rich with the whole of her
youth instead of distributing it to many in pennyworths. He
warns her of the perils of a lost reputation, a warning which,
if she was what he thinks she is, would surely come too late.
Marcella pretends to disagree with what he says, and leaves
him, boasting that she will spend her gold, not hoard it.
Mr. Galliard next has to encounter difficulties. The chaste
Marcella pretended to Sir Harry that she was wanton. Now
the wanton Cornelia pretends to Mr. Galliard that she is chaste.
He refuses to believe her preposterous tale, as he thinks it, that
she is not the courtesan she seems to be, but a young virgin of
quality. Their inconclusive exchange, in which Cornelia defends
from Mr. Galliard the principle of constant love which she
attacked in Marcella, leaves them both dissatisfied. Mr.
Galliard says: "Oh the impudence of honesty and quality in
women! A plague on them both, they have undone me." But
secretly Cornelia too laments her display of virtue: "Now o' my
conscience, there never came good of this troublesome virtue."[36]
Cornelia wears one mask over another. She is a girl of lax
morality, posing as a girl of strict morality disguised as a girl of
lax morality.

Therefore Mr. Galliard, in despair, seeks another mistress.
Restoration Comedy is plentiful in sharp, vivid portrayals of
jealousy: the jealousy of Pinchwife and Manly in Wycherley,
for example, or of Mrs. Termagant in Shadwell or of Amanda
in Vanbrugh; the jealousy of Loveit, when she pushes Dorimant
away from Bellinda: "Stand off, you shall not stare upon her
so."[37] Jealousy lies near the heart of *The Way of the World*, and
is the life-breath of *The Double Dealer*. Cornelia, in her tears at
Mr. Galliard's desertion of her, exclaims of his new mistress:
"His lady! Oh blast her, how fair she is!" Her suffering is
another of Mrs. Behn's arguments in favour of constant love.
But because of all the confusions Mr. Galliard fails to seduce
anyone that night; so, crying, "So many disappointments in

one night would make a man turn honest in spite of nature,"
he decides to marry Cornelia. The girls explain—unflatteringly
—that they disguised themselves as courtesans to be sure of
meeting Sir Harry, Sir Harry marries Marcella, and constant
love prevails.

Dryden's chief contributions to the debate between constant
and inconstant love are to be found in *Marriage à la Mode* and
Secret Love, two comedies which are as colossally and impres-
sively lifeless as stuffed whales. Dryden differed from Aphra
Behn in greeting marriage, even between people in love, with
at the best an uneasy and mistrustful acquiescence. His own
wife, Lady Elizabeth Howard, gave him reason to inveigh
frequently against the wedded state all his life. Dryden must
readily have accepted the definition of marriage by his contemporary, Samuel Butler:

> A Happiness that only Lyes
> Amonge the Sottish or the wise
> That oversee, or else Prevent
> Th'occasions of their Discontent.[38]

Palamede, in the impassively lewd *Marriage à la Mode*, woos
Rhodophil's wife, Rhodophil woos Palamede's mistress, all
unknown to each other. Each man wants both the women.
Each woman wants both the men. The craftily carpentered
dénouement comes when both couples keep an assignation
outside a grotto at the same time. Rhodophil throughout the
play voices a vivid discontent with the institution of matrimony.
He is oppressed by the dread of habit and regularity which is
recognised in Etherege's *The Comical Revenge*, especially in the
course of the scene during which Sir Frederick Frollick seren-
ades the widow.

WIDOW. Sir *Frederick*, is it you?

SIR FRED. Yes truly; and can you be angry, Lady? Have not your
Quarters been beaten up at these most seasonable hours before
now?

WIDOW. Yes; but it has been by one that has had a Commission
for what he did: I'm afraid shou'd it once become your Duty,
you would soon grow weary of the Employment.[39]

Rhodophil feels the repugnance for a settled condition expressed in another of Etherege's plays, *She Would If She Could*. To him, as to Sir Oliver Cockwood, all lawful solace is abomination. That Rhodophil's wife Doralice shares her husband's estimate of marriage is denoted by her song, "Why should a foolish Marriage Vow?"

Rhodophil says he has, by smelling the same strong perfume for two years, sickened of the scent. "The fashion of great beds", he claims, "was invented to keep husband and wife sufficiently asunder." During a quarrel with Doralice he accuses her of having blunted his faculties:

> I was never thought dull till I marry'd thee; and now thou hast made an old knife of me, thou hast whetted me so long, till I have no edge left.[40]

He is convinced that "There's something of antipathy in the word marriage to the nature of love." Not much cheered by the experience of his friend Rhodophil, Palamede looks upon his own approaching marriage with dread, and decides upon one last illicit skirmish:

> A little comfort from a Mistris, before a man is going to give himself in Marriage, is as good as a lusty dose of Strong-water to a dying Malefactour.[41]

But the mistress whom Palamede chances upon is Doralice, who bores Rhodophil so much. Rhodophil in turn seeks stimulation in Melantha, Palamede's future wife.

By accident Doralice's honour is saved by the encounter at the grotto, but Rhodophil and Palamede agree, on principle, to fight. Doralice is obliged to reason them out of their conduct. It then strikes Rhodophil that if his friend, whose judgement he respects, loves Doralice, there must be something more in her than he himself has found; whilst Palamede concedes:

> Here's an argument for me to love *Melantha*; for he has lov'd her, and he has wit too, and, for aught I know, there may be a Mine; but, if there be, I am resolv'd I'll dig for't.[42]

The jealousy brought about by these reflections gives the friends, in Doralice's words, "the most delicate sharp sauce to a cloyed stomach". In conclusion, Rhodophil and Palamede draw up a covenant not to invade each other's property; with a clause that "whoever breaks the league, either by war abroad, or by neglect at home, both the women shall revenge themselves, by the help of the other party".[43]

Celadon and Florimel, in Dryden's earlier play, *Secret Love, or the Maiden Queen*, are avowed inconstants. Celadon is a light-hearted and voluble young man who makes a cult of variety in his loves. "Marriage", he says, "is poor folk's pleasure, that cannot go to the cost of variety."[44] He says that he cannot be faithful to only one mistress. He asks for a hundred of them, since he has more love than any one woman can deal with. He meets Florimel, to whom he boasts of his fickleness, and is delighted to find her equally capricious:

> FLORIMEL. For what an unreasonable thing it were to stay long, be troublesome, and hinder a Lady of a fresh Lover.
> CELADON. A rare Creature this![45]

But Celadon falls sincerely in love with Florimel:

> FLORIMEL. But, without raillery, are you in Love?
> CELADON. So horribly much, that contrary to my own maxims, I think in my Conscience I could marry you.[46]

She demands proofs of love from him—heroic extremes: "You will grant it is but decent you should be pale, and lean, and melancholic, to shew you are in love." Celadon rightly guesses that "a treat, a song and the fiddles" are more acceptable proofs of love to Florimel. Those proofs and the alarming question, "Dost thou know what it is to be an old Maid?", persuade her to change her views on love and marry Celadon. For the "rich old rogue", as Celadon calls his father, they will provide:

> Grandchildren in abundance, and great Grandchildren upon them, and so inch him and shove him out of the world by the very force of new Generations.[47]

Shadwell's *Epsom Wells* suggests a likelier solution to the problem of marital incompatibility than that offered in *Marriage à la Mode*. On the subject of marriage, Shadwell, as is usual with him, is neither quite decorous nor quite licentious. His first play, *The Sullen Lovers*, ends with a most unpromising marriage. The world-weary Stanford tries to live like a hermit in his Covent Garden lodging, but is intruded upon by various impertinent people. His already vexed nerves are further irritated by the procession of the dogmatic Sir Positive At-all, self-admiring poet Ninny, the coxcomb Woodcock, and the cadger Huffe; each of whom is less a character than an iteration. To escape them, he marries Emilia, a young woman as morose and unsociable as himself, and goes to hide in the country. Much of the humour, such as it is, of the play lies in the ungraceful courtship of the misanthropic lovers. One doubts whether a marriage between a bad-tempered man and a bad-tempered girl is likely to be a sweet one. One is reminded of Tennyson's remark about the marriage of the Carlyles: that it was a good thing, inasmuch as it made only two people unhappy instead of four. Thus Shadwell diverges from Molière, whom he has been loosely imitating up to this point. Shadwell's Alceste-Stanford takes with him into his retirement the worst potential trouble of them all.[48] *The Sullen Lovers* is wound up unconventionally, with Emilia's complaints about the fuss of the wedding, Stanford's proposal to withdraw to a "distant desert", and no great hopes of future happiness.

Shadwell deserves credit at least for the originality of his endings. *Epsom Wells* culminates not in a marriage but in an unmarriage, with Mr. Woodly and his wife agreeing to separate:

> When Man and Wife no more each other please,
> They may at least like us each other ease.[49]

Mr. and Mrs. Woodly announce their agreement: their first agreement, Mrs. Woodly thinks, since their wedding. Woodly declares that he will separate from Mrs. Woodly for ever. Mrs. Woodly, who claims that for two years she has seldom seen her husband by daylight, adds that his "lewd disorderly life" has already caused an effective separation. All marital obligations shall cease between them. Woodly shall keep whatever mistresses he pleases, and how he pleases. Mrs. Woodly shall have no spies upon her company or behaviour:

> WOODLY. And if at any time I should be in drink, or otherwise in a loving fit, and should be desirous to visit you, it shall and may be lawful for you to deny me ingress, egress and regress.
> MRS. WOODLY. Yes, though you serve me as you do others, and break my Windows.
> WOODLY. I restore you all your Portion, and add 2000 l. to it for the use I have had on you.
> MRS. WOODLY. So, it is done.[50]

It would not be too much to say that *Epsom Wells* was written, at a time when divorce was obtainable only by a special Act of Parliament, in favour of easier laws of divorce. Amanda, in Cibber's *Love's Last Shift* and Vanbrugh's *The Relapse*, has no redress against the infidelities of her husband, except the discreditable one of becoming an adultress herself. In *The Provoked Wife* Vanbrugh further considers the difficulties of a woman with a vicious husband, and once again rejects adultery as their solution. The social purpose of *The Provoked Wife* is twofold. Firstly, it is a hint to all potential Sir John Brutes concerning the consequences which their behaviour may bring upon them. Secondly, it presents evidence for the desirability of divorce in such scenes as the one in which Sir John Brute, dirty, bloody from his brawls, stinking of drink, and disappointed in his search for a prostitute, comes home and kisses and tumbles the wife who is so much in his power. *The Provoked Wife*, and to a less extent *The Relapse*, imply that the proper remedy for matrimonial ills is divorce. To that extent they may be regarded as advocating a reform in the morals of the time.

"What cloying meat is love", exclaims Sir John Brute, repeating Rhodophil's sentiments in *Marriage à la Mode*, "when matrimony's the sauce to it". Two years' marriage in his view, has debauched his senses, so that they are all tainted with his wife:

No Boy was ever so weary of his Tutor, no Girl of her Bib, no Nun of doing Penance nor Old Maid of being chast, as I am of being Married. Sure there's a secret Curse entailed upon the very Name of Wife.[51]

Confronted with Sir John's sexual repletion, it is no wonder that Mr. Constant considers that marriage excludes people from the obligations of faithfulness:

Constancy's a brave, free, haughty, generous Agent, that cannot buckle to the Chains of Wedlock. There's a poor sordid Slavery in Marriage, that turns the flowing Tide of Honour, and sinks us to the lowest ebb of Infamy.[52]

The weightiest part of Farquhar's *The Beaux' Stratagem* concerns, not the two young heroes Archer and Aimwell, but the unhappy marriage of Mr. and Mrs. Sullen, who are in some measure modelled on Sir John and Lady Brute. Mrs. Sullen is a London heiress who detests the countryside and is married to a drunken landowner of Lichfield. As she says, they are "united contradictions, fire and water".[53] Farquhar had been reading Milton's divorce-pamphlets with an earnest attention presumably prompted by the failure of his own marriage. Several scenes in *The Beaux' Stratagem* echo passages in the pamphlets. Sometimes Farquhar uses Milton's own words. Of an incompatible marriage Milton had written in Book II of *The Doctrine and Discipline of Divorce*:

Nay instead of being one flesh, they will be rather two carkasses chain'd unnaturally together; as it may happ'n, a living soule bound to a dead corps.[54]

Farquhar renders these words in dramatic form:

SULLEN. You're impertinent.
MRS. SULLEN. I was ever so, since I became one flesh with you.
SULLEN. One flesh! Rather two carcasses joined unnaturally together.
MRS. SULLEN. Or rather a living soul coupled to a dead body.[55]

Milton wrote that God did not authorise a "judicial court to toss about and divulge the unaccountable and secret reasons of disaffection between man and wife, as a thing improperly answerable to any such kind of trial".[56] Mrs. Sullen elaborates upon this:

> What law can search into the remote abyss of Nature, what evidence can prove the unaccountable disaffections of wedlock? Can a jury sum up the endless aversions which are rooted in our souls, or can a bench give judgement upon antipathies?

Milton had advocated divorce by mutual consent: "There is no power above their own consent to hinder them from unjoining. . . . Not he who puts away by mutual consent commits adultery." Farquhar ends *The Beaux' Stratagem*, as Shadwell does *Epsom Wells*, with such a divorce by mutual consent:

> Both happy in their several States we find,
> Those parted by consent, and those conjoin'd.
> Consent, if mutual, saves the Lawyer's fee;
> Consent is Law enough to set you free.[57]

In that final snatch of verse the dying Farquhar affirmed his belief in a preventive for all the adulteries which take place in Restoration Comedy.

EPILOGUE

FARQUHAR'S LAST PLAY was published in 1707. The ritual obsequies of the Restoration drama were performed in 1709, when the company at Drury Lane deserted the theatre-owner, Christopher Rich, and moved in a body to Vanbrugh's theatre in the Haymarket. They lowered the ceiling, and reduced the width of the auditorium, so that at last the words spoken on the stage could be heard in the arrogant Baroque distances of that disastrously beautiful interior. A new company obtained a licence to re-open the Drury Lane theatre, but Rich sabotaged them. He stripped the theatre of all its movables and sold them, leaving the new company "nothing but an empty stage, full of trapdoors known only to himself and his adherents".[1] Sir Richard Steele in *The Tatler* gave a comic inventory of the effects for sale from the defunct theatre: three bottles and a half of lightning; one shower of snow in the whitest French paper; two showers of a browner sort; a dozen and a half of clouds, streaked with black and well-conditioned; a setting sun, a pennyworth; a new moon, something decayed; a rainbow, a little faded.[2] Under the rainbow, a little faded, Restoration Comedy was buried like Beardsley's Salome, in a powder-box coffin with a powder-puff for a lid.

The epitaph was already written by John Dryden, who had ushered in the age and was, by general consent, its Master of Ceremonies; and had died in the early part of 1700. He concluded his *Secular Masque*, first performed at Drury Lane two nights before his death, with lines which make the best ending to our account:

> All, all of a piece throughout;
> Thy chase had a Beast in view;
> Thy wars brought nothing about;
> Thy lovers were all untrue.
> 'Tis well an old Age is out,
> And time to begin a new.[3]

A morning not its own had filled the Restoration theatre with its light, stripping of their glamorous incertitudes the chalk-streaked planks, the dust-swimming proscenium, the fabrics rubbed bare, the rouge on the jutting cheek-bones and the sweat on the wrinkled faces. The convention had been sustained for long enough. Its vitality was exhausted:

> Ash on an old man's sleeve
> Is all the ash the burnt roses leave.
> Dust in the air suspended
> Marks the place where a story ended.[4]

The men of mode and the men of honour, the rakes and the fops, the valets and the double-dealers, the ladies of quality and the furious trapped harlots, paled under their disguises in that dawn, as the gods in Wagner's *Rhinegold* pale when the giants carry off the goddess of youth.

NOTES
BIBLIOGRAPHY
CHRONOLOGY

F

N.B.

In the body of the text the familiar modern spellings of titles are given. In the following Notes original spellings are used throughout.

NOTES TO CHAPTERS

Chapter 1: Cupid's Fav'rite Nation

1. *Astræa Redux*. ll. 250–5. Dryden: *Poems*, I, p. 22
2. Pepys, I, p. 149 (25 May, 1660). The painting, by Verrio (*James II* Catal. No. 57), at present hangs in the Queen's Presence Chamber.
3. Pepys, I, p. 145 (23 May, 1660).
4. ibid., I, p. 150 (25 May, 1660).
5. idem.
6. Pepys, I, p. 161 (8 June, 1660).
7. ibid., I, p. 254 (2 November, 1660).
8. See Bryant: *Charles II*, p. 82.
9. Pepys, I, p. 245 (20 October, 1660).
10. Butler: *Hudibras*, p. 8:
    Rather than fail, they will defy
    That which they love most tenderly;
    Quarrel with Minc'd-Pies, and disparage
    Their best and dearest Friend Plum-Porridge;
    Fat Pig and Goose itself oppose,
    And blaspheme Custard thro' the Nose. (I, i. 225–30)
11. Pepys, II, p. 399 (26 December, 1662).
12. ibid., III, p. 30 (4 February, 1663).
13. Milton: *Works*, IV, pp. 317–18:
    If we think to regulat Printing, thereby to rectifie manners, we must regulat all recreations and pastimes, all that is delightfull to man. No musick must be heard, no song be set or sung, but what is grave and *Dorick*. There must be licencing dancers, that no gesture, motion, or deportment be taught our youth, but what by their allowance shall be thought honest. . . . It will ask more than the work of twenty licencers to examin all the lutes, the violins, and the ghittarrs in every house; they must not be suffer'd to prattle as they doe, but must be licenc'd what they may say. And who shall silence all the airs and madrigalls that whisper softnes in chambers. . . . The villages also must have their visitors to enquire what lectures the bagpipe and the rebbeck reads, ev'n to the ballatry, and the gamuth of every *municipal* fidler. . . . Our garments also should be referr'd to the licencing of some more sober workmasters to see them cut into a lesse wanton garb.

14. Inderwick: *Interregnum*, pp. 33 and 36.
15. ibid., p. 39.
16. ibid., p. 55.
17. ibid., p. 45.
18. ibid., pp. 46–7.
19. ibid., p. 55.
20. Aubrey, II, p. 304.
21. Pepys, III, p. 179 (1 July, 1663).
22. Rochester: Antwerp *Poems*, p. 14.
23. Milton: *Paradise Lost*, I, 498–502.
24. For the influence of Fletcher see Smith: *The Gay Couple*.
25. Summers: *Restoration Theatre*, pp. 212 et seq.
26. ibid., p. 235.
27. *Sir Patient Fancy*, III, ix.
28. Pepys, II, p. 119 (28 October, 1661).
29. ibid., III, p. 48 (23 February, 1663).
30. Nicoll: *Restoration Drama*, p. 18.
31. Vanbrugh: *Complete Works*, I, p. 12.
32. Summers: *Restoration Theatre*, p. 259.
33. Nicoll: *Restoration Drama*, p. 259.
34. Ham: *Otway & Lee*, pp. 185–6.
35. Genest: *English Stage*, I, pp. 427–8.
36. Boswell: *Court Stage*, pp. 130–1.
37. Roscommon: *Works*, p. III. Hor. A.P., 396–401.
38. Etherege: *Plays*, II, p. 185. The Prologue is by Sir Car Scroope.
39. ibid., p. 288.
40. To this effect Congreve himself writes in his *Letter concerning Humour in Comedy. Complete Works*, III, pp. 162–3.
41. Shadwell: *Complete Works*, I, p. 101.
42. Dryden: *Poems*, II, p. 577.
43. *Un Voyage à Cythère. Fleurs du Mal*, p. 121.
44. Burnet: *Rochester*, p. 12.
45. Aubrey, II, p. 304.
46. Pinto: *Rochester*, pp. 250–1.
47. *Letter from Artemisia*, ll. 63–4. *Poems*, p. 81.
48. *The Town Fop*, IV.iii.
49. Perromat: *Wycherley*, p. 103.
50. *The Tatler*, No. 3 (14 April, 1709).
51. *The Country Wife*, II.i.
52. ibid., V.i.
53. ibid., III.ii.
54. *The Way of the World*, V.xiii.
55. Preface to *State of Innocence* (1677); Perromat: *Wycherley*, p. 104.
56. *The Plain Dealer*, I.i.

57. *An Allusion to Horace*, l. 43. *Poems*, p. 96.

58. *A Satyr against Mankind*, ll. 135–6. *Poems*, p. 122. Several Rochester scholars (e.g. Pinto and Brooks) hold that *Rochester's Farewell* may be by Rochester, with later interpolations.

59. William Empson: *Missing Dates. Collected Poems*, p. 60. I am grateful to Professor Empson for his permission to quote from this poem.

60. Johnson: *Lives* I, p. 221.

Chapter 2: The Sons of Belial

1. Etherege: *Letterbook*, pp. 2 et seq.; T.L.S., 16.2.1922; N. and Q., 6–27.5.1932.

2. *Letterbook*, pp. 5 and 207; *Biographia Britannica*, III, pp. 1841 and 1844.

3. *Letterbook*, pp. 11–12; Hatton Correspondence, I, p. 133.

4. *Letterbook*, pp. 8–9; *Biographia Britannica*, III, p. 1844.

5. *Letterbook*, pp. 14–15; B.M. Harleian MS. 162; *Biographia Britannica*, III, p. 1844.

6. *Letterbook*, p. 16; P.R.O. Signet Office Doquets, 6817.

7. *Letterbook*, pp. 378–9.

8. ibid., pp. 379 and 382–3.

9. ibid., p. 58.

10. ibid., p. 389.

11. Shadwell: *Complete Works*, I, pp. xvii–xx; Borgman, pp. 6 and 11; *Biographia Britannica*, VI, p. 3624. For a very just critical revaluation of Shadwell see Sutherland, pp. 120–5.

12. Lines 457–509.

13. *Complete Works*, V, p. 265.

14. *The Address of John Dryden. Complete Works*, V, pp. 349 ff.

15. *Biographia Britannica*, VI, p. 3626; George Saintsbury's Introduction to Mermaid ed. of Shadwell's select plays, p. xvi.

16. By Dryden in his *Vindication of the Duke of Guise*. Dryden: *Works*, VIII, p. 180.

17. See the Dramatis Personae of, e.g., *The Scourers* and *Epsom-Wells*.

18. In a memoir "by one of the Fair Sex" prefixed to Behn: *Histories & Novels*, at p. 2. Because Lady Winchilsea, writing in about 1695, said that Aphra Behn's father was a barber of Wye in Kent, and because the baptismal register at Wye records the baptism of Ayfara, daughter of John Amis, on 10 July, 1640, Montagu Summers (Behn: *Works*, I, pp. xvii–xviii) concludes that her maiden name was Amis. But the burial register at Wye records the burial of Afara, daughter of

John Amis, on 12 July, 1640 (Link: *Aphra Behn*, p. 18). Thus the authority of the earliest biography has not here been replaced by something better.

19. Behn: *Histories & Novels*, pp. 2–3 and 152–4.

20. ibid., pp. 5 ff.; Behn: *Works*, I, pp. xx–xxvii; St. P. July–December, 1666; Cameron: *New Light On A.B.*, pp. 34 et seq.

21. Behn: *Miscellany*, p. 75; Behn: *Works*, I, pp. xxxiiii–xxxiv.

22. *Bibliotheca Hoyleana*. The sale took place at Richard's Coffee House in Fleet Street on 14 November, 1692. Among the philosophers represented were Lucretius, Hobbes and Spinoza. The classical works, as in Congreve's library, were mostly in Latin, although there were some bilingual editions in Latin and Greek; also a Greek-Latin dictionary. There were two editions each of Martial and Suetonius. Hoyle is reputed to have had a hand in Aphra Behn's comedies (Behn: *Works*, I, p. xxxiv).

23. Luttrell, I, p. 395 (see also II, p. 464); Behn: *Works*, I, p. xxxv. There is no record of the proceedings Luttrell mentions in the copy of the Session Papers at the Guildhall Library; but a note, "The Grand Jury returned Ignoramus on another" (Proceedings of the King's Commissioners in the Old Bailey, 23–25 February, 1687).

24. Behn. *Works*, I, pp. xlii–xliii; *Protestant Mercury*, 12.8.1682; Woodcock: *Incomparable Aphra*, p. 162.

25. *On Mr Dryden, Renegade*. Behn: *Works*, VI, p. 400.

26. Behn: *Works*, III, p. 187.

27. ibid., I, pp. lii–lvii.

28. *Love-letters to a Gentleman* in Behn: *Histories & Novels*. See Sackville-West: *Aphra Behn*, pp. 52–5, for an enthusiastic account. The portrait is reproduced as a frontispiece to Behn: *Works*, I.

29. *The Feign'd Curtezans*, V.ii.

30. Wycherley: *Complete Works*, I, pp. 7–8; *The Plain-Dealer*, I.i.

31. Spence: *Anecdotes*, I, p. 322.

32. Spence: *Anecdotes*, I, p. 33; Dennis: *Critical Works*, II, p. 409.

33. Wood: *Athenae Oxoniensis*, IV, p. 527.

34. idem.

35. *The Country Wife*, IV.i.

36. Wycherley: *Complete Works*, III, *pp.* 187–8 and I, 17.

37. Spence: *Anecdotes*, I, p. 321.

38. *Love in a Wood*, V.v.

39. Wycherley: *Complete Works*, I, pp. 35–6; Spence: op. cit., I, p. 34: Cibber: *Lives*, III, pp. 249 et seq.: Macaulay, II, p. 426.

40. Spence: op cit., I, p. 245.

41. ibid., I, p. 33.
42. Wycherley: *Complete Works*, I, p. 37.
43. ibid., I, pp. 37–8; Dennis: *Familiar Letters*, pp. 217 ff.
44. Wycherley: *Complete Works*, I, p. 53; Spence: *Anecdotes*, I, pp. 35 and 38.
45. Spence: op cit., I, pp. 321–2; Connely: *Brawny Wycherley*, pp. 148 and 160–1.
46. Spence: op. cit., I, p. 321.
47. Wycherley: *Complete Works*, I, p. 55.
48. Griffith: *Chronicles*, p. 149.
49. Gildon: *Memoirs*, p. 7.
50. *The Third Pastoral* (*Autumn*). See Spence: op. cit., I, p. 41 and Perromat: *Wycherley*, pp. 62 ff.
51. Spence: *Anecdotes*, I, p. 39; Pope: *Letters* (21.1.1716).
52. Johnson: *Lives*, II, p. 213. Congreve's surname is rhymed, in an epigram of the time, with "one grave".
53. Hodges: *Congreve*, p. 17.
54. Johnson: *Lives*, II, p. 213.
55. Hodges: *Letters & Documents*, p. 216.
56. Congreve: *Works*, III, p. 182.
57. ibid., II. p. 9.
58. Hodges: *Congreve*, pp. 98–9.
59. ibid., pp. 83–7 et passim; Johnson: *Lives*, II, pp. 225–6; *Biographia Britannica*, II, p. 1448.
60. Dryden wrote of his "entire affection" for Congreve (Hodges: *Letters & Documents*, p. 89). Addison solicited papers for *The Spectator*. Steele dedicated his *Miscellany* to him, and Pope his *Iliad*, calling Congreve the last of the Romans (ibid., pp. 219 and 233–4).
61. Johnson: *Lives*, II, pp. 217–18.
62. Congreve: *Works*, IV, p. 42.
63. Hodges: *Congreve*, p. 49.
64. Hodges: *Letters & Documents*, pp. 19 and 106.
65. In a letter to John Dennis, 11.8.1695 (Hodges: *Letters & Documents*, p. 188). Dennis had written (ibid., p. 186) that Congreve could not have been more forgetful of his correspondents, had the Tunbridge Wells waters sprung from Lethe.
66. *The Mourning Bride*, III.vi.
67. ibid., II.iii.
68. Collier: *Short View*, pp. 42 and 44.
69. ibid., p. 38.
70. ibid., pp. 92–3.
71. Vanbrugh: *Complete Works*, I, p. 196.
72. Congreve: *Amendments*, p. 4.

73. ibid., p. 5
74. Congreve: *Works*, III, p. 198. Congreve seems to have suspected some schoolmasters of erotic cruelty, since he accuses Collier of lashing the stage "as a sinful pedagogue sometimes lashes a pretty boy, that looks lovely in his eyes, for reasons best known to himself: Castigo te, non quod odio habeam sed quod amem".
75. Congreve: *Amendments*, p. 1.
76. Hazlitt: *Comic Writers*, p. 95.
77. Johnson: *Lives*, II, p. 227.
78. Spence: *Anecdotes*, I, pp. 324–5; Hodges: *Congreve*, pp. 78 and 116–20.
79. Hodges: *Letters & Documents*, pp. 238 and 248–9.
80. ibid., pp. 265 and 268–9.
81. ibid., pp. 250, 264 and 268.
82. Whistler: *Vanbrugh*, pp. 14 and 16. Vanbrugh's mother, however, was the daughter of Sir Dudley Carleton, nephew of Viscount Dorchester. Vanbrugh: *Complete Works*, I, p. lxii.
83. Whistler: *Vanbrugh*, pp. 24–7
84. Collier: *Short View*, p. 79.
85. Vanbrugh: *Complete Works*, I, p. 206.
86. Cibber: *Apology*, pp. 172–4.
87. Vanbrugh: *Complete Works*, I, p. xiv.
88. ibid., IV, p. xi.
89. Hodges: *Congreve*, p. 116.
90. Swift: *Poems*, I, p. 78.
91. Swift: *Journal to Stella*, 31.10.1710.
92. Whistler: *Vanbrugh*, p. 123.
93. Walpole: *Anecdotes*, p. 310.
94. Whistler: *Vanbrugh*, p. 116.
95. Vanbrugh: *Complete Works*, I, p. xxx.
96. ibid., IV, p. 107.
97. ibid., IV, p. 111.
98. ibid., IV, p. 146.
99. *The Constant Couple*, I.ii.
100. ibid., I.ii.
101. Farquhar: *Complete Works*, II, p. 279.
102. Baker: *Biographia Dramatica*, I, p. 225.
103. Farquhar: *Complete Works*, I, p. 86.
104. idem.
105. Farquhar: Dublin *Works*, I, p. xi.
106. *Complete Works*, II, p. 192; Connely: *Farquhar*, p. 296.
107. Farquhar: *Complete Works*, I, p. xxxi; Chetwood: *History*, p. 152.
108. *Complete Works*. II, p. 359.

Chapter 3: Mode and Honour

1. Matthew Bramble's letter of 23 April.
2. *The Rivals*, I.ii.
3. Pepys, II, p. 400 (27 December, 1662).
4. *The Comical Revenge*, I.xv and III.vi.
5. *Sir Patient Fancy*, V.i.
6. *Epsom-Wells*, I.i.
7. *The Old Batchelor*, IV. iv.
8. Xenophon: *Constitution of Sparta*, V.
9. *Love in a Wood*, III.i.
10. *The Constant Couple*, II.iv.
11. *She wou'd if she cou'd.* I.ii.
12. Hamilton: *Grammont*, p. 187.
13. ibid., p. 262.
14. *The Way of the World*, III.xv.
15. *The Man of Mode*, V.ii.
16. ibid., V.i.
17. *The Gentleman Dancing-Master*, II.ii.
18. ibid., I.i.
19. *The Sullen Lovers*, IV.i.
20. *Epsom-Wells*, II.i.
21. *The Squire of Alsatia*, I.i.
22. *Bury-Fair*, III.i.
23. *The Beaux' Stratagem*, II.i.
24. *Love for Love*, II.x.
25. ibid., II.xi.
26. ibid., III.vii.
27. ibid., V.iv.
28. ibid., V.vi.
29. ibid., V.x.
30. *The Way of the World*, V.xiv.
31. *The Double-Dealer*, I.ii.
32. *The Man of Mode*, II.i.
33. *The Provok'd Wife*, II.i.
34. *Bury-Fair*, II.i.
35. Temple: *The Gardens of Epicurus*, p. 62.
36. *The Sullen Lovers*, II.i.
37. *The Comical Revenge*, IV.iv and V.ii.
38. *The Country-Wife*, V.iv.
39. idem.
40. Wycherley: *Complete Works*, IV. p. 128.
41. *The Country-Wife*, IV.i.
42. *Epsom-Wells*, I.ii.

43. *Song to Chloris. Works of Celebrated Authors*, I, p. 201.
44. *Epsom-Wells*, II.i.
45. *The Town-Fop*, II.iii.
46. ibid., IV.iii.
47. ibid., V.iv.
48. *Love in a Wood*, I.ii.
49. ibid., II.i.
50. ibid., V.vi.
51. *The Squire of Alsatia*, V.i.
52. idem.
53. ibid., II.i.
54. *The Gentleman Dancing-Master*, I.ii; Aristophanes: *The Clouds*, ll. 958 et seq.
55. *Marriage à la Mode*, III.i.
56. *The Provok'd Wife*, I.ii.
57. *Bury-Fair*, III.i.
58. *The Way of the World*, IV.i.
59. *Love's Last Shift*, I.i.
60. ibid., III.i.
61. idem.
62. ibid., V.ii.
63. *The Relapse*, I.i.
64. idem.
65. ibid., V.iv.
66. *Sir Harry Wildair*, V.vi.
67. ibid., V.ii.
68. *The Feign'd Curtezans* was produced in 1679, and *The City Heiress* in 1682. Wilding, the hero of *The City Heiress*, has affinities with Bellmour, the hero of *The Town-Fop* of 1677.
69. *The City Heiress*, I.i.
70. ibid., II.iii.
71. ibid., III.i. and IV.ii.
72. ibid., V.v.

Chapter 4: I am my Own Fever

1. *The Plain-Dealer*, I.i.
2. Wycherley: *Complete Works*, II, pp. 101–2.
3. *The Plain Dealer*, IV.i.
4. idem.
5. idem.
6. Morley: *Character Writings*, p. 210.

7. *The Gentleman Dancing-Master*, IV.i. See Perromat, pp. 106 et seq., for a discussion of the source, which Wycherley has greatly improved upon.
8. ibid., I.i.
9. *The Country-Wife*, III.i.
10. *The Double-Dealer*, III.i.
11. ibid., V.xviii.
12. ibid., IV.xvii.
13. ibid., I.vi.
14. ibid., IV.xviii.
15. ibid., III. iv.
16. ibid., IV.ii.
17. *The Gentleman Dancing-Master*, II.ii.
18. *The Double-Dealer*, V.iv.
19. ibid., IV.i.
20. *Love for Love*, IV.xvi.
21. *The Town Fop*, III.iii.
22. ibid., IV. iii.
23. *A True Widow*, II.i.
24. ibid., III.i.
25. ibid., IV.i.
26. ibid., III.i.
27. ibid., V.i.
28. Traherne: *Centuries*, III.i–ii.
29. Shadwell: *Complete Works*, I, p. 91.
30. *The Way of the World*, III.v.
31. *The Comical Revenge*, V.v.
32. ibid., I.ii.
33. ibid., III.ii.
34. ibid., V.v.
35. idem.
36. *Love in a Wood*, I.i.
37. *Epsom-Wells*, IV.i.
38. *The Way of the World*, IV.v. The humorous marriage-contract is also used in Dryden's *Secret Love* (1667) and in Edward Ravenscroft's *Careless Lovers* (1673). Ravenscroft adds a provision against "calling names". Fulsome endearments are satirised in *The Man of Mode*, *Epsom-Wells*, *The Country-Wife* and *The Old Batchelor*. See Smith's *The Gay Couple*.
39. *Sir Patient Fancy*, II.i.
40. idem.
41. idem.
42. ibid., III.iii.
43. idem.

44. *The Old Batchelor*, IV.xxii.
45. Juvenal., X, 28–35.
46. *The Old Batchelor*, I.iv.
47. ibid., III.x.
48. *The Virtuoso*, IV.i.
49. *Parny: Élégies*, IV.viii.
50. *The Doubler-Dealer*, I.vi.
51. ibid., IV.vi.
52. ibid., III.i.
53. ibid., I.iii.
54. ibid., II.i.
55. ibid., III.iii.
56. ibid., V.xvii.
57. *The Old Batchelor*, II.ix.
58. Dryden: *Works* (ed. Swedenberg), VIII, p. 327. *The Indian Queen* (operatic version), III.ii. Professor James Kinsley very much doubts that this song was written by Dryden himself, and excludes it from his edition of Dryden's poems.

Chapter 5: *My Heart is the Pendulum*

1. Preface to *Miscellany Poems*, II. Dryden: *Poems*, I, pp. 396–7.
2. Creech, I, p. 199.
3. *To Mr. Creech on his Translation of Lucretius*. Creech, I, sig. (b); Waller: *Poems*, II, p. 91.
4. *To Mr. Creech on his Accurate Version for Lucretius*. Creech, I, sig. (b2).
5. *To his Ingenious Friend Mr. Creech on his Excellent Translation of Lucretius*. Creech, I, sig. (a) verso.
6. *To Mr Creech upon his Translation of Lucretius*. Creech, I, sig. (a2).
7. *To the unknown Daphnis on his Excellent Translation of Lucretius*. Creech, I, sig. (a2) verso.
8. idem.
9. Behn: *Miscellany*, p. 75. That Congreve was also a great admirer is suggested by the presence in his library of four editions of Lucretius, one of them with Creech's notes. In addition Congreve owned the works of Saint-Évremond and a six-volume abridgement of Gassendi. Hodges: *Library of Congreve*, pp. 48, 53 and 64–5. Bellmour, in *The Old Batchelor*, protests in Epicurean terms: "Leave business to idlers and wisdom to fools" (I.i.). Cf. Millamant's rebuke ("Idle creature") when Mirabell mentions his early rising (*W. of W.*, IV.v).
10. Charleton: *Epicurus's Morals*, p. 23.

11. *Ce fameux épicurien . . . faisait profession d'un luxe poli et n'avait que des voluptés étudiées.* Sarasin: *Œuvres*, II, p. 54.

12. Saint-Évremond: *Letters* (ed. Hayward), p. 274.

13. Virgil draws upon this account in his Sixth Bucolic, especially in ll. 31–40.

14. Virg. Georg., II, 490–3; Dryden: *Poems*, II, p. 955.

15. Charleton: *Epicurus's Morals*, I, p. 15.

16. Lecky: *European Morals*, I, p. 76.

17. Charleton: *Epicurus's Morals*, sig. d4r.

18. Creech, I, p. 146; Lucretius, II, 646–51 (erroneously duplicated in Book I in seventeenth-century editions).

19. Rochester: *Poems*, p. 50.

20. Creech, I, p. 147; Lucr., II, 652–7.

21. Lucr., III, 944–62. *Eadem sunt omnia semper.*

22. Creech, I, p. 276.

23. ibid., I, p. 274; Lucr., III, 1011–13.

24. idem. Seneca paraphrased Lucretius's lines in part of a Chorus of his *Troades* (ll. 379–408). Rochester's loose translation of this chorus-ending (*Poems*, p. 49) is noble in its forthrightness.

25. Hobbes: *Leviathan*, I.xiv.

26. Charleton: *Darkness of Atheism*, pp. 96–7.

27. Charleton: *Epicurus's Morals*, pp. 14–15.

28. Traherne: *Centuries*, III.xlvi.

29. Evelyn: *Lucretius*, sig. 6v; letter to Casaubon, 15 July, 1674.

30. In two successive works: *De vita et moribus Epicuri*, 1647; and *Philosophiae Epicuri syntagma* (appended to Gassendi's commentary on Diogenes Laertius), 1649.

31. *Letters* (ed. Hayward), p. 33.

32. ibid., p. xliv.

33. *Lettres* (ed. Ternois), I, pp. 269 and 288.

34. *Œuvres en Prose*, III, p. 430.

35. *Lettres* (ed. Hayward), p. 279.

36. Spence: *Anecdotes*, I, p. 221.

37. Etherege: *Letterbook*, p. 264 (original in French).

38. *Love for Love*, IV. xx.

39. *She wou'd if she cou'd*, I.i.

40. ibid., IV.ii.

41. ibid., I.i.

42. *The Man of Mode*, III.iii.

43. Hobbes: *Leviathan*, I.xiii.

44. *Tyrannic Love*, III.i. Dryden dissents from Lucretius in the preface to *Miscellany Poems*, II. Dryden: *Poems*, I, pp. 395–6.

45. *The Virtuoso*, I.i.

46. *The Country-Wife*, I.i.

47. ibid., V.iv.
48. ibid., IV.iv.
49. ibid., IV.iii.
50. *The Gentleman Dancing-Master*, V.i.
51. *The Constant Couple*, II.v.
52. ibid., I.iii.
53. ibid., II.iii.
54. ibid., V.i.
55. *Mon Cœur Mis à Nu*, III, IX and XIII. Baudelaire: *Journaux Intimes*, pp. 53–64.
56. *L'Art Romantique*, pp. 89–91.
57. *The Relapse*, I.iii.
58. Browne: *Religio Medici*, p. 252. In *Religio Medici*, Part II, Browne attempts a defence of Epicurean philosophy.
59. *The Relapse*, II.i.
60. ibid., III.i.
61. idem.
62. ibid., IV.v.
63. ibid., IV.iv.
64. ibid., V.v.
65. *Love's Last Shift*, I.i.
66. ibid., II.i.
67. ibid., III.i.
68. idem.
69. *The Careless Husband*, II.ii.
70. ibid., V.vii.
71. ibid., II.ii.

Chapter 6: *Bright Nymphs of Britain*

1. Behn: *Works*, IV, pp. 115–16.
2. Behn: *Feign'd Curtezans*, I.i. and II.i.
3. *She wou'd if she cou'd*, I.ii.
4. *The Man of Mode*, III.i.
5. ibid., V.ii.
6. *The Virtuoso*, I.i.
7. *The Squire of Alsatia*, III.i.
8. *Bury-Fair*, III.i.
9. *The Gentleman Dancing-Master*, II.i.
10. idem.
11. ibid., V.i.
12. *The Relapse*, II.i.

13. ibid., III.ii.
14. ibid., II.i.
15. *The Provok'd Wife*, III.i.
16. ibid., III.iii.
17. *The Recruiting Officer*, V.i.
18. ibid., V.ii.
19. *The Way of the World*, IV.v.
20. *The Old Batchelor*, IV.xi.
21. *The Man of Mode*, V.ii.
22. *The Provok'd Wife*, III.i.
23. *The Forsaken Mistress*. Etherege: *Poems*, p. 3.
24. *The Man of Mode*, V.ii.
25. *The Country-Wife*, I.i.
26. ibid., III.i.
27. *The Plain-Dealer*, II.i.
28. idem.
29. *King Arthur*, II.ii. *Poems*, II, p. 570.
30. idem.
31. idem.
32. *The Feign'd Curtezans*, I.i.
33. ibid., II.i.
34. ibid., II.i. and III.i.
35. ibid., IV.i.
36. ibid., IV.ii.
37. *The Man of Mode*, II.ii.
38. Butler: *Satires & Miscellanies*, pp. 213 and 219.
39. *The Comical Revenge*, III.ii.
40. *Marriage à la Mode*, III.i.
41. ibid., V.i.
42. idem.
43. idem.
44. *Secret Love*, I.i.
45. ibid., I.ii.
46. ibid., II.i.
47. ibid., III.i.
48. *The Sullen Lovers*, V.i.
49. Shadwell: *Complete Works*, II, p. 181.
50. *Epsom-Wells*, V.i.
51. *The Provok'd Wife*, I.i.
52. ibid., III.i.
53. *The Beaux' Stratagem*, II.i.
54. Milton: *Works*, III, p. 478. See Connely: *Farquhar*, pp. 282 and 331.
55. *The Beaux' Stratagem*, III.iii.

56. Milton: *Works*, III, p. 498.
57. *The Beaux' Stratagem*, V.iv.

Epilogue

1. *Tatler*, No. 99 (26 November, 1709).
2. ibid., No. 42 (16 July, 1709).
3. Dryden: *Poems*, IV, p. 1764.
4. *Little Gidding*, Eliot: *Poems and Plays*, p. 192.

BIBLIOGRAPHY

1. *Principal Texts*
Aphra BEHN: *Works*. Ed. Summers. London, 1915.
Colley CIBBER: *The Careless Husband*. London, 1735.
—— *Love's Last Shift*. London, 1735.
William CONGREVE: *Complete Works*. Ed. Summers. London, 1923.
John DRYDEN: *Works*. Ed. Swedenberg and Dearing. Berkeley and
    Los Angeles, 1956–.
Sir George ETHEREGE: *Plays*. Ed. Brett-Smith. Oxford, 1927.
George FARQUHAR: *Complete Works*. Ed. Stonehill. London, 1930.
Thomas SHADWELL: *Complete Works*. Ed. Summers. London, 1927.
Sir John VANBRUGH: *Complete Works*. Ed. Dobrée and Webb.
    London, 1927.
William WYCHERLEY: *Complete Works*. Ed. Summers. London, 1924.

2. *Other Works cited in the Notes*
ARISTOPHANES: *Works*. Ed. Rogers. London and Cambridge, Mass.,
    1960–3.
John AUBREY: *Brief Lives*, Ed. Clark. Oxford, 1898.
D. E. BAKER: *Biographia Dramatica*. London, 1812.
Charles BAUDELAIRE: *L'Art Romantique*. Ed. Crépet. Paris, 1925.
—— *Les Fleurs du Mal*. Ed. Starkie. Oxford, 1953.
—— *Journaux Intimes*. Ed. Crépet and Bein. Paris, 1949.
Aphra BEHN: *Histories and Novels*. London, 1735.
—— *Miscellany*. London, 1685.
BIOGRAPHIA BRITANNICA. London, 1747–66.
A. S. BORGMAN: *Thomas Shadwell*. New York, 1928.
Eleanore BOSWELL: *The Restoration Court Stage*. Harvard, 1932.
Sir Thomas BROWNE: *Religio Medici*, London, 1906.
Sir Arthur BRYANT: *Charles II*. London, 1931.
Gilbert BURNET, Bishop of Salisbury: *Some Passages in the Life and
    Death of John, Earl of Rochester*. London, 1680.
Samuel BUTLER: *Hudibras*. Ed. Wilders. Oxford, 1967.
—— *Satires and Miscellanies*. Ed. Lamar. Cambridge, 1928.
W. J. CAMERON: *New Light on Aphra Behn*. Auckland, 1961.
Walter CHARLETON: *The Darkness of Atheism Discovered*. London, 1652.
—— *Epicurus's Morals Collected and Englished*. London, 1926.
W. R. CHETWOOD: *General History of the Stage*. London, 1749.
Colley CIBBER: *An Apology for the Life of Colley Cibber*. Ed. Fane.
    Michigan, 1968.

Theophilus CIBBER: *Lives of the Poets*. London, 1753.

Jeremy COLLIER: *A Short View of the Immorality and Profaneness of the English Stage*. London, 1730.

William CONGREVE: *Amendments of Mr. Collier's False and Imperfect Citations*. London, 1698.

Willard CONNELY: *Brawny Wycherley*. London, 1930.

—— *Young George Farquhar.* London, 1949.

Thomas CREECH: *Lucretius, Of the Nature of Things Translated into English Verse*. London, 1714.

John DENNIS: *Critical Works*. Ed. Hooker. Baltimore, 1939–43.

—— *Familiar Letters*. London, 1696.

DIOGENES Laertius: *De vitis clarorum philosophorum*. Ed. Hicks. London and New York, 1925.

John DRYDEN: *Miscellany Poems*, London, 1684.

—— *Poems*. Ed. Kinsley. Oxford, 1958.

—— *Works*. Ed. Scott and Saintsbury. Edinburgh, 1882–92.

T. S. ELIOT: *Complete Poems and Plays*. London, 1969.

William EMPSOM: *Collected Poems*. London, 1950.

Sir George ETHEREGE: *The Letterbook*. Ed. Rosenfeld. Oxford, 1928.

—— *Poems*. Ed. Thorpe. Princeton, 1963.

John EVELYN: *The First Book of Lucretius Englished*. London, 1656.

George FARQUHAR: *Works*. Dublin, 1775.

Pierre GASSENDI: *De vita et moribus Epicuri*. Paris, 1647.

John GENEST: *Some Account of the English Stage*. Bath, 1832.

Charles GILDON: *Memoirs of the Life of William Wycherley*. London, 1718.

A. GRIFFITH: *Chronicles of Newgate*. London, 1884.

R. G. HAM: *Otway and Lee*. New Haven, 1931.

Anthony HAMILTON, known as Anthony, Count Hamilton: *Memoirs of the Count de Gramont*. Ed. Scott. London, 1846.

HATTON LETTERS: *Correspondence of the Family of Hatton, 1601–1704*. London, 1878.

William HAZLITT: *Lectures on the English Comic Writers*. Ed. Brimley Johnson. London, 1907.

Thomas HOBBES: *Leviathan*. Ed. Lindsay. London, 1914.

J. C. HODGES: *William Congreve the Man*. New York and London, 1941.

J. C. HODGES (ed.): *The Library of William Congreve*. New York, 1955.

—— *William Congreve: Letters and Documents*. London, 1964.

John HOYLE: *Bibliotheca Hoyleana: sive catalogus variorum librorum Johannis Hoyle*. London, 1692.

F. A. INDERWICK: *The Interregnum*. London, 1891.

Samuel JOHNSON: *Lives of the English Poets*. Ed. Birkbeck Hill. Oxford, 1905.

JUVENAL: *D. Junii Juvenalis satirae XIII*. Ed. Mayor. London and
    New York, 1888–9.
W. E. H. LECKY: *History of European Morals*. London, 1911.
F. M. LINK: *Aphra Behn*. New York, 1968.
LUCRETIUS: *T. Lucreti Cari de rerum natura libri sex*. Ed. Munro.
    Cambridge, 1893.
Narcissus LUTTRELL: *A Brief Historical Relation*. Oxford, 1857.
Thomas Babington, Lord MACAULAY: *Essays*. Ed. Grieve, London,
    1907.
Thomas MIDDLETON: *Plays*. Ed. Ellis. London, 1887.
John MILTON: *Works*. Ed. Patterson. New York, 1931–40.
Henry MORLEY (ed.): *Character Writings of the Seventeenth Century*.
    London, 1891.
Allardyce NICOLL: *History of Restoration Drama*. Cambridge, 1923.
Évariste-Désiré de Forges, Vicomte de PARNY: *Œuvres*. Ed. Pons.
    Paris, 1873.
Samuel PEPYS: *The Diary*. Ed. Wheatley. London, 1904.
Charles PERROMAT: *William Wycherley, sa vie, son œuvre*. Paris, 1921.
V. de Sola PINTO: *Rochester*. London, 1935.
Alexander POPE: *Letters*. Ed. Butt. London, 1960.
John Wilmot, Earl of ROCHESTER: *Poems*. Ed. Sola Pinto. London,
    1964.
—— *Poems on Several Occasions*. "Antwerp", 1680(?).
Wentworth Dillon, Earl of ROSCOMMON: *Works*. Glasgow, 1753.
Charles Marguetel de Saint-Denis, seigneur de SAINT-ÉVREMOND:
    Letters. Ed. Hayward. London, 1930.
—— *Letters*. Ed. Ternois. Paris, 1967.
—— *Œuvres en Prose*. Ed. Ternois. Paris, 1966.
Jean François SARASIN: *Œuvres*. Ed. Festugière. Paris, 1926.
SENECA: *Tragedies*. Ed. Miller. London and New York, 1917.
Richard Brinsley SHERIDAN: *Plays and Poems*. Ed. Crompton Rhodes.
    Oxford, 1928.
J. H. SMITH: *The Gay Couple in Restoration Comedy*. Harvard, 1948.
Tobias George SMOLLETT: *Humphry Clinker*. London, 1771.
Joseph SPENCE: *Anecdotes of Men and Books*. Ed. Osborn. Oxford,
    1966.
Montagu SUMMERS: *The Restoration Theatre*. London, 1934.
James SUTHERLAND: *English Literature of the Late Seventeenth Century*
    (O.H.E.L., VI). Oxford, 1969.
Jonathan SWIFT: *Journal to Stella*. Ed. Ryland. London, 1900.
—— *Poems*. Ed. Mitford. London, 1833.
The TATLER: London, 1797.
Sir William TEMPLE: *The Gardens of Epicurus*. Ed. Forbes Sieveking.
    London, 1908.

Thomas TRAHERNE: *Centuries, Poems and Thanksgivings*. Ed. Margoliouth. Oxford, 1958.

VIRGIL: *P. Vergili Maronis Opera*. Ed. Connington and Nettleship. London, 1875–81.

Edmund WALLER: *Poems*. Ed. Thorn Drury, London, 1893.

Horace WALPOLE: *Anecdotes of Painting*. London, 1879.

V. Sackville-WEST: *Aphra Behn*. London, 1927.

Laurence WHISTLER: *Sir John Vanbrugh*. London, 1938.

Anthony à WOOD: *Athenae Oxoniensis*. Ed. Bliss. London, 1813–20.

George WOODCOCK: *The Incomparable Aphra*. London, 1948.

WORKS OF CELEBRATED AUTHORS. London, 1750.

XENOPHON: *Scripta Minora*. Ed. Marchant. London and New York, 1925.

CHRONOLOGY

1660 The Restoration. Dryden's *Astraea Redux*. Pepys began diary. Establishment of Royal Society. Bunyan imprisoned.
1661 Molière's *Les Fâcheux*. Versailles begun.
1662 Part One of Butler's *Hudibras*. Molière's *L'École des femmes*.
1663 Dryden's *Wild Gallant* produced. Cowley's *Occasional Verses*.
1664 Etherege's *Comical Revenge* produced and published. Howard and Dryden's *Indian Queen* produced. Waller's *Poems*.
1665 *Indian Queen* published. The Great Plague. Naval war with Holland. La Rochefoucauld's *Maximes*.
1666 Bunyan's *Grace Abounding*. Fire of London. Molière's *Le Misanthrope*.
1667 Milton's *Paradise Lost*. Dryden's *Secret Love* produced. Death of Cowley.
1668 Etherege's *She Would If She Could* and Shadwell's *Sullen Lovers* produced and published. *Secret Love* published. Dryden's *Essay of Dramatic Poesy*. Dryden poet-laureate.
1669 Dryden's *Tyrannic Love* produced. *Wild Gallant* published.
1670 Behn's *Forced Marriage* produced. *Tyrannic Love* published.
1671 *Rehearsal* and Wycherley's *Love in a Wood* produced. *Forced Marriage* published.
1672 Wycherley's *Gentleman Dancing Master*, Dryden's *Marriage à la Mode*, and Shadwell's *Epsom Wells* produced. *Rehearsal* and *Love in a Wood* published.
1673 Behn's *Dutch Lover* produced and published. *Gentleman Dancing Master*, *Marriage à la Mode* and *Epsom Wells* published.
1674 Deaths of Milton and Traherne.
1675 Wycherley's *Country Wife* produced and published.
1676 Etherege's *Man of Mode* and Shadwell's *Virtuoso* produced and published. Behn's *Town Fop* and Wycherley's *Plain Dealer* produced.
1677 Dryden's *All for Love* produced. *Town Fop* and *Plain Dealer* published. Death of Spinoza.
1678 Behn's *Sir Patient Fancy* produced and published. Shadwell's *A True Widow* produced. *All for Love* published. Bunyan's *Pilgrim's Progress*. Popish plot.
1679 Behn's *Feigned Courtesans* produced and published. *A True Widow* published.
1680 Rochester's "Antwerp" *Poems?* Temple's *Miscellanea*. Deaths of Rochester and Lely.

1681 Part One of *Absalom and Achitophel*. Oldham's *Satires upon the Jesuits*.

1682 Otway's *Venice Preserved* and Behn's *City Heiress* produced and published. Creech's Lucretius.

1683 Dryden's Plutarch. Siege of Vienna.

1685 Death of Charles II. Crowne's *Sir Courtly Nice* produced and published.

1686 Behn's *Lucky Chance* produced.

1687 *Lucky Chance* published. Dryden's *Hind and the Panther*.

1688 Shadwell's *Squire of Alsatia* produced and published. Glorious Revolution. Birth of Pope.

1689 Shadwell's *Bury Fair* produced and published. Tate and Purcell's *Dido and Aeneas* first performed. William & Mary.

1690 Locke's *Essay concerning Human Understanding*.

1691 Dryden and Purcell's *King Arthur* produced and published. Congreve's *Incognita*. Death of Etherege.

1692 Settle and Purcell's *Fairy Queen* produced and published. Shadwell's *Volunteers* produced. Death of Shadwell.

1693 Congreve's *Old Bachelor* produced and published and *Double Dealer* produced. *Volunteers* published.

1694 *Double Dealer* published. Death of Queen Mary.

1695 Congreve's *Love for Love* produced and published.

1696 Cibber's *Love's Last Shift* produced and published. Vanbrugh's *Relapse* produced.

1697 Vanbrugh's *Provoked Wife* produced and published. *Relapse* published. Congreve's *Mourning Bride* produced and published.

1698 Farquhar's *Love and a Bottle* produced. Collier's *Short View*.

1699 Farquhar's *Constant Couple* produced and published. *Love and a Bottle* published.

1700 Congreve's *Way of the World* and Dryden's *Secular Masque* produced and published. Death of Dryden.

1701 Farquhar's *Sir Harry Wildair* produced and published.

1704 Cibber's *Careless Husband* produced.

1705 *Careless Husband* published.

1706 Farquhar's *Recruiting Officer* produced and published.

1707 Farquhar's *Beaux' Stratagem* produced and published. Death of Farquhar.

N.B. The authority for the dates of production is *The London Stage, 1600–1800* (Illinois, 1960–8), Part I (ed. van Lennep) and Part II (ed. Avery).

INDEX

INDEX